EGYPT VS. GREECE

GREECE

and the American Academy

T0149864

Molefi Kete Asante and Ama Mazama
Temple University

Editors

Chicago, Illinois

Front Cover illustration by
Ed Bunch and John Stubblefield

Copyright © 2002 by
Molefi Kete Asante and Ama Mazama

First Edition, First Printing

Printed in the United States of America

ISBN: 0-913543-77-2

EGYPT VS. GREECE
and the American Academy

TABLE OF CONTENTS

iii

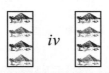

ACKNOWLEDGEMENTS

We would like to thank Ana Yenenga and Garvey Lundy for the strong support and encouragement they have given us while we worked on this project. We dedicate this work to the memory of Cheikh Anta Diop who did so much to redirect the historiography of Africa. We would like to make a special acknowledgement of Dr. Jawanza Kunjufu who works tirelessly to create opportunities for intellectual discourse around our liberation.

A Discourse on Cultural and Social Knowledge
Molefi Kete Asante and Ama Mazama

Kemet, Greece, China, Axum, and India may be the most significant civilizations of antiquity. However, in the Western world, Egypt and Greece have played dominant roles in the construction of science, philosophy and social ethics. Since the rise of European triumphalism during the 15th century there has been a persistent encroachment upon the cultural and social spaces of other people. Maghan Keita, writing in his recent book, *Race and the Writing of History*, has argued the validity of viewing history from different perspectives. Along with the European physical and political incursions into the realms of others went intellectual colonization to the degree that information was structured to support European hegemony.

In the past twenty years the field of Africology has developed innovative approaches to apprehending African phenomena. One of the most important perspectives in this regard is Afrocentricity. The Afrocentrists have begun a campaign to re-envision the history of Africa and the African relationship to Europe. Accepting Cheikh Anta Diop's suggestion to tie the study of all African civilizations to the classical Nile Valley, many contemporary scholars have opened new avenues for human knowledge. Thus, the discovery in Nigeria, near Ilorin, of nearly two thousand stone sculptures, called the Esie carvings, that represent one of the largest caches of ancient carvings ever found and the discovery of a canoe more than 8000 years old push back the antiquity of Western Africa.

The continent, quite frankly, has yet to be discovered in a thorough and systematic way. The anecdotal and trivial journalism of numerous European writers, and lately, a few Africans from America, have meant that the nature of the discourse around Africa has been colored by European arrogance and lack of serious reflection. One way to redress this situation is to examine the data we have from an Afrocentric point of view. We have attempted to give the public and scholars a book that meets all of the demands of contemporary scholarship but one that radically reconstructs the orientation to data.

The history of African American Studies as a discipline is recent, beginning with the establishment of the doctoral program at Temple University in 1987. Prior to that time African American Studies was essentially a collection of courses about African people with no specific theories, methods, or objectives apart from those that had been defined by traditional European disciplines. Consequently those teaching in African American Studies were often the children of Eurocentric ontological, cosmological, epistemological and axiological parents. Indeed, many followed Eurocentric aesthetics as well. Out of this context a core of faculty at Temple University, the Temple Circle as it was called in the literature, sought to develop African American Studies as a discipline with particular language and assumptions. Africology, a name suggested by Winston Van Horne, and his colleagues at the University of Wisconsin-Milwaukee, had presented itself as the proper name of the discipline.

Our objective in this volume is to present the Africological discourse on the classical relationship between Egypt and Greece in a way that enlightens rather than obscures the facts. Since Africology is the Afrocentric study of African phenomena, what we are concerned with in a concrete and practical manner is the examination of the relationship cultural orientation has to information.

This is a sensitive subject because there are some European writers who believe that to suggest that the Greeks were but children to the Egyptians is anathema to scholarship. They are convinced that basic to all modern knowledge is Greek philosophy and science. Usually the European writers begin with the discussion of the sixth century B.C philosophers Thales, Pythagoras, Anaximander, and Isocrates and their successors. Through the centuries Europe developed for itself a self-conscious attitude toward its own culture and organized its own approaches to the world. While the first contact between the Egyptians and Greeks came when the Greeks studied and traveled in Egypt, it would be the age of European imperialism that would seek to change the relationship of Greece to Egypt as a hierarchical one with Greece occupying the central place.

We have assembled in this volume authors whose purpose is to shed light on the historiography of this relationship, describe its dimensions and scope, and suggest the ethical ideas upon which the Africological discipline should continue to hold discourse on this subject. Of course African American Studies, or as we prefer Africology, is not a closed field and there exists no uniformity in the opinions and ideas of the writers who are presented in this volume. What does exist in these essays as a common thread, however, is the overarching concern with centering Africans within the phenomenological context so as to view Greece as an equal, not superior partner in the making of modern society. Such a task as this implies language, terminology, paradigms, metatheories, and constructions of a scientific nature that involve information and ideas from other disciplines. But the path of development in these essays is toward the discipline of Africology.

It is important to say this at the outset, that the writers in this volume are interested in setting the record straight and re-ordering the discussion about Egypt, that is, Africa, and Greece, that is, Europe, in antiquity. The ignorant might call this necessary reassessment "mythmaking" but the scholar's role, if anything, is to question, re-evaluate, and present facts. When one considers the fact that the Egyptian philosophers such as Imhotep, Amenhotep, son of Hapu, Kagemni, Amenemhat, and Amenomope and others are never discussed in European writings on ancient philosophy, it is easy to understand why so many Afrocentric scholars are eager to open the door to those closed chambers. We are delighted that a few of them have joined in our discourse in this volume.

The scholars chosen for this volume are among the most prolific writers dealing with the nature of European hegemony in cultural and social thought. In a sense they are exploring the roots of human civilization seeking to reconstruct ancient history according to the rationality of the factual evidence. These are not political manifestoes but rather they are analytical and historical essays interrogating the fundamental relationship between culture and society, particularly as this relationship impinges upon the understanding of African realities. We invite a lively discussion and debate rather than the often-shrill voices of those who have stood too long on the uncertain sand of a Eurocentric hegemony in human knowledge.

Those who declare competence in the discipline of Africology ought to be familiar with the classical foundations of the field, speak the same language, observe the rituals of criticism and analysis and possess an understanding of the ethical dimension of seeking to break the bonds of oppression in all forms. This is the minimum set of conditions for someone to claim to be a part of the discipline. It is indeed a litmus test but it is not unlike the criteria in other fields for such declarations of discipline.

The origin of African thought about medicine, astronomy, ethics, religion, and morals is in the Nile Valley. Similarly, European thought finds its origin in the Greek isles. Under the radical criticism of Afrocentricity the Greek miracle has been shown to be non-existent inasmuch as the Greek achievements had to be seen as parts of the African project along the banks of the Nile. Egypt rises around 3400 B.C. and Greece around 1000 B.C. Not only was Egypt prior to Greece in chronology it was the teacher of the earliest Greek philosophers: Thales, Pythagoras, Isocrates, and others.

We present this volume as a contribution to the on-going intellectual re-assessment of antiquity in order to understand who we are, where we are going, and how we are to get there. So many contradictions exist in the current literature of the ancient world that it is quite useful that Afrocentric scholars have come together to challenge, but not only to challenge, to actually set aright what has been missing in the discourse on the classical world. As the philosopher Maulana Karenga has urged, we must constantly study to determine how to model ideas" from an ongoing synthesis of the best in African culture" (Karenga, 2001). This is no easy road because it will pass through territories that have seldom been traveled in the American academy. Yet it brings the type of intellectual thrill that gives us hope that human commonality and goodwill might prevail in the academy and in the world.

One more point, we recognize that even in the name of our book, *EGYPT VS. GREECE and the American Academy*, we have given ground to the Greek's influence on the nature of our discourse. Our consciousness of using Kemet and Egypt interchangeably should not confuse the reader; we see the Greek name of the ancient African land as one of the legacies that must be changed one day on the ground as well as in the literature. Because we are in the period of transition you will see both Kemet and Egypt used in this book. Each of the authors who write for this volume recognizes the antiquity of the name Kemet. They have only used Egypt, where they have used it, to insure that modern readers will understand the meaning of their work. We have followed them in this convention.

Reference

Maulana Karenga, *Kawaida Theory*. Los Angeles: University of Sankore Press, 1998.

Locating the Eurocentric Assumptions about African History
Molefi Kete Asante
Temple University

There are certain premises and positions that have become untenable by virtue of the Afrocentric intervention into social sciences and humanities. Afrocentrists have opened doors to historical research that have been long held shut by Eurocentric orientations to phenomena. For instance, in ancient historiography few scholars are now willing to take ancient Egypt out of Africa as Hegel, Breasted, and Maspero tried to do in the 19th and early part of the 20th century (Hegel, 1982; Breasted, 1917; Maspero, 1911). No serious researcher would claim, as Toynbee did, that Africa produced no civilizations (Toynbee, 1987).

Almost no one would argue the positions advanced by Fage concerning African people (Fage, 1969). While a few Whites can still be found who preach the inferiority of Africans, almost no scholar would be foolhardy enough to suggest that Whites are biologically superior to Blacks. In fact, I have witnessed a remarkable change in attitude on the part of many White scholars who are now following the tradition of Afrocentrists in their examination of phenomena by taking into greater consideration oral traditions, centered analysis, human similarities, and locational analysis, spheres previously examined mainly by Afrocentrists.

My aim is to demonstrate the explanatory power of the Afrocentric paradigm. I do not aim to present a litany of interpretative achievements. I have defined Afrocentricity as a perspective on phenomena that views African people as subjects rather than objects. This means that all analyses of African phenomena must be seen in the light of Africans as actors not mere spectators to Europe. Such a slight alteration in perspective produces new understandings and advancement in science. Afrocentricity is therefore in the perspectivist tradition. Assuming, as I do, that intellectual

location is central to interpretation the Afrocentrist seeks to examine phenomena from a particular place. Intellectual location is
the psychological and historical space occupied by an observer
of phenomena. This space I refer to as *place*. While it is true that
place is significant in such an interpretative design it is not *place*
alone that enables the scholar to make a proper analysis. However,
you cannot have an orientation to the facts that leads in the direction
of explanation if you are badly located, that is, if you are misplaced.

For instance, there was almost no possibility that a White
southern medical doctor would adequately and correctly diag-
nose African patients during slavery. Doctors were poorly placed
to draw the proper conclusion from what they saw. In her pen-
etrating Afrocentric study *Slavery and Medicine*, Katherine
Bankole examined slave medicine only to find that the doctors
who tended to Africans were often so influenced by the system of
White supremacy that they viewed all African illness in the context of White superiority and Black inferiority (Bankole, 1997).

The assumptions that caused doctors to misdiagnose Africans were based on attitudes about slavery. How could an African want anything other than slavery? Thus, any African who
ran away from the plantation had to be suffering from a particularly bad form of *drapetomania*, the desire to leave forced labor.
If the African happened to show a dislike for slavery and the
overseer or master of the plantation, he or she was diagnosed as
having *rascality,* a disease of Africans who are irritated by their
environment.

A recent African American history book written by a committee for high schools claims that during the 1840s the White
slave owners had a problem because so many Africans were running away. There is a problem in such construction from the
Afrocentrist's point of view because it is impossible to accept the
marginalizing of Africans. I am particularly radicalized by the
authors' lack of respect for the people who were actually having
a problem, the Africans.

In another instance we are confronted with the shining models of the American drive for democracy: The Declaration of Independence, the Federalist papers and the Constitutional conventions in Philadelphia. What do we know about the Africans' response to these instruments of nation building? Did White historians really care to ask? What were the Africans' positions on these subjects during the course of debates and conclusions? Why were their voices not recorded in the earlier documents and not discussed in the history books? Did they not have a voice? Does this say something about the White supremacist location of the Founding White Fathers? It is probably more beneficial to look at the White historians' location for an answer to how they interpreted the Africans' presence or lack of presence in colonial America. What does it mean that historians have rarely speculated, as Ray Winbush, opined in *Black Issues in Higher Education* (1996) on the nature of the discussions among the servants, horsemen, and cooks who assisted the White conventioneers with personal services during their meetings on the nature of the new government?

What can it mean that a whole generation of European scholars sought, while claiming to be Egyptologists to undermine the African nature of ancient Egypt? While there was some criticism by Whites of this project, why did not the mass of historians object to the blatant racism in the early formulation of ancient African history? Those early Egyptologists sought to take Egypt out of Africa and Black skinned Africans out of Egypt. It was a conspiracy to minimize African's role in early human civilization. Such a conspiracy could only be carried out because of the near uniform belief among Whites in the inferiority of Africans. The Great Enslavement of Africans had seen to it that Whites developed and maintained negative attitudes about African history and capability. What purposes and whose interests were served by the steady denial of the Blackness of the ancient Egyptians? All one has to do is to examine the record and it will be clear that these scholars present a complex argument against an African Egypt. They do this despite the overwhelming nature of the facts. Location becomes the critical issue, that is, the only interpretative issue. Let it be clear the question of the Blackness of the ancient Egyptians would never have been raised except for the persistent White racism in Western history. It had not been an issue in Europe prior to the 15th century and only became an issue with the vast discoveries in Egypt during the 19th century, a most imperialistic century for Europe.

Audrey Smedley has written brilliantly about the origins of racism making the point that the concept of "race" was designed with its ideological fabrications about human differences to be used as a mechanism for maintaining "distant" and "social status place" of various peoples (Smedley, 1998). Race, thus established, became an instrument for determining who should have power, authority, prestige, agency, and independence. It was a status marker, restricting competition while the practitioners of racism argued for competition in a contradictory and hypocritical manner. It is no wonder that the historians born of this context held some of the same beliefs as the masses of Whites. They saw Africans as morally, intellectually, physically, and culturally inferior to Whites. It is easy to see how people who had devised such elaborate intellectual contortions as race would have a problem believing that "low status" people could have constructed the monuments of ancient Egypt.

Who could these African people who produced the greatest civilization of antiquity be? Surely in the minds of the early European scholars there had to be an explanation that showed them to be different from Africans who lived in societies contiguous to Egypt. In the eyes of those whose culture was warped by slave trading and colonization the ancient Egyptians could not be Africans, after all Europeans were enslaving Africans! If they admitted that the Egyptians were Africans they would have to declare that they were not Black. They had to be White Africans! Who during the 19th century would believe that Blacks built the pyramids? What Whites of the 19th century could admit that fact? In a curious ways Whites of the 20th century have argued the same point but with a different twist. They ask, why do Africans want to claim Egypt? Why not claim West Africa? The obvious answer is that both are Africa, but the question itself remains a throwback to the canard about Egypt not being Africa. Egypt and Nubia impacted on the rest of Africa as thoroughly as China impacted on parts of Asia, or Greece impacted on parts of Europe.

Because Europe was working out its own relationship to its past during the last five hundred years, the historians of the West captured the ambiguity present in Europe's own wrestling with its diversity. When they spoke of Africans, they largely defined a narrow idea of a "true Negro" that usually referred to Africans from the rainforest region of the continent that had come to mean for Whites, primitive, dangerous, mysterious, and the extreme of themselves physically. To satisfy their stereotypes they took physical characteristics such as the shape of lips, the width of the nose, and the size of genitalia to be definitive statements about the difference between themselves and Africans. Surely the ancient Egyptians could not be Africans. It is as if Africans would say that the only Europeans are the Scandinavians who are extremely pale, with red or blond hair, long noses, and a love of the sea. This was a wicked ideology maintained as science by some of the leading European scholars.

In effect, the ideology of White supremacy was the rocket engine that put into flight the fantastic ideas of a White Egypt, buttressed by one self-serving Egyptologists after another. The Nile Valley civilization arising about 3400 B.C. in historical terms and ending with the Romans dispossession around 50 B.C. did not evolve in isolation from the rest of Africa. Egypt was rather clearly an African civilization as connected to Africa's history and geography as Axum or Nubia. The fact of the Blackness of the ancient Egyptians was accepted in Europe during the Renaissance. Actually

11

prior to 1830 it was generally understood that the ancient Egyptians were Black. However, after 1830, that is, after the Champollion's deciphering of the *Medu Netcher* and the publication of Dominic Vivant Denon's *Description of Egypt,* came the attempt to take Egypt out of Africa. Some authors have argued that the racism that produced this type of negative attitude toward Black achievements was born during the slave trade as an attempt to justify morally what Whites were doing to Africans physically. Few interpretative histories of European Slave Trade have dealt with the ideology of White supremacy as a generating force for much of the anti-African historiography (Asante, 1998).

Egypt in the Mind of Modern Europeans

The objections to an Afrocentric historiography of Africa range from the frivolous to the serious. I place those who argue from the old racist paradigm in the category of the frivolous because they seek to argue by dismissal, to refute by ignorance, rather than engage the concrete arguments of the Afrocentric historians. The serious but off-center writers would include Frank Snowden and his followers like Frank Yurco. Snowden has become the standard bearer for an out-of-date, off-centeredness that borders on the marginalization of Africans in their own history. They are serious scholars, however, because they engage data but off-center because they assume a European *place*, a European centrality while discussing Egypt and Nubia. Both civilizations predate Greece and to make them dance around Greece is turning the tables on their heads. Snowden does this in his often-cited book, *Blacks in Antiquity.* As I have often pointed out in discussion, Snowden's idea is not about Blacks in Antiquity but about Blacks in the minds and thoughts of the Greeks and Romans. The Africans Snowden sees are like stones, they cannot speak for themselves, and they only become important because they are picked up by either the Greeks or the Romans. This is a strange and dangerous intellectual interpretation of African data.

"Locating the Eurocentric Assumptions about African History"
Molefi Kete Asante
Temple University

An argument of the frivolous school is that the ancient Egyptians were not Black and not Africans. Of course, the Egyptians were both Black and African; neither fact is difficult to determine or to observe historically, geographically, culturally, or linguistically. If we mean by African a person or people whose historical cultural antecedents are in the continent of Africa no one can deny that the ancient Egyptians, so-called Pharaonic Egyptians, were Africans. It is, by the way, frivolous, almost ludicrous, to argue as David Kelley argued that the White South Africans who come to the United States ought to be called Africans Americans. The Whites of South Africa find their historical antecedents in Europe and in European cultures, not in Africa. Indeed their more recent domicile in Africa did little to erase their understanding of themselves as culturally different from Africans people among whom they lived. Had they been Africans in the historical sense the past sixty years in South Africa would have been quite different. The fact that they were Europeans who believed in White supremacy led directly to their problems with Africans.

Now in a prehistoric sense science confirms the African origin of humanity and in that regard we may be said to all be Africans. However, in the period of history, where signs and symbols have created unique articulations of our experiences with environment and other humans, and where our responses have been reflected in art, writing, architecture, designs, clothes, structures of governance, and motifs of thought and behavior. Differentiation has created distinct and unique human communities. We do not have the same specific cultures or histories although in palter of concentric lines we might be able to interpret our specific experiences from the smallest unit to larger units until we embrace the world. This is why it is necessary for a scientific historiography to distinguish the imaginary from the real, the illusion from the concrete. Thus, the ancient Kemites, Egyptians if you will, were African people. They reflected the same responses to history as their continental neighbors and for the most part knew little outside of the Nile valley.

Secondly, they were black skinned people even during the rather late period when the Greeks came to Egypt to study and travel. The Greeks saw the Egyptians as black skinned and the most common word used to describe the Egyptians' color was *melanchroes,* black skinned. Had the Greeks wanted to describe them as white they would have used *leucochroes* but they did not. Neither did they say *phrenychroes*, which is brown or red skinned. The very use of the word *melanchroes* from the same root for words such as melanin, melanite, Melanesia, and so forth meant that there was no confusion or complex in the mind of either the Herodotus or Aristotle on this subject. I am the first to admit that both may have been bad scientists on some subjects but on the people they actually saw with their own eyes I find them credible. As to the historical method it is better to accept the witness of these ancient Greeks than late 20th century interpreters. Aristotle says in *Physiognomonica* that the Egyptians and Ethiopians are very Black. This passage is translated in the Loeb as "too Black" indicating that Aristotle saw the Ethiopians, Greek for burnt faces, and the Egyptians as Black skinned people. He did not say the Ethiopians are "too Black" but rather that both of them were very Black (Aristotle, *Physiognomonica*).

Aristotle's commentary was made prior to the Greek invasion of Africa under Alexander the Macedonian and during the end of a period begun around the 6th century B.C. when Thales of Miletus had entered school in Egypt. Thales studied philosophy in Egypt and subsequently became the first Greek philosopher. Aristotle is usually called one of the major Greek writers but rarely has he been quoted on the color of the Ethiopians and Egyptians. An observation on the complexion of the Egyptians made in the 4th century B.C. is sufficient to call into question in late 20th century argument to the contrary regarding the ancient Egyptians. Indeed no implication is necessary when we recall the two statements made by Herodotus in the second book of Histories.

"Locating the Eurocentric Assumptions about African History"
Molefi Kete Asante
Temple University

Herodotus claims that the people of Colchis, wherever it was located near the Black Sea and whatever its history was in reference to Egyptian conquerors, looked like the Egyptians. But what is the reason why this 5th century Greek historian makes such a definite claim that the Colchians are descended from the Egyptians? He writes that they are "Black skinned and have wooly hair" (Herodotus, *Book II*). This is not the description of a European person or an Asian person. Herodotus has come under patricidal declamations by European historians who once called him the Father of History but who increasingly find him problematic. Of course, Herodotus was a product of his time and was limited in his scope and often wrote things that were fanciful. The complexion of the ancient Egyptians was not fanciful, however. In fact he knew precisely what he was talking about and although a few translators have used the term "dark skinned" for Herodotus' description of the ancient Egyptians most admit that melanchroes is Black skinned. It is good to remember that Herodotus had no bones to crack on this issue. He did not have the consciousness of contemporary Europeans. Africans had not been victims of enslavement and had not been deprived of heritage and history. When Herodotus wrote his book, Alexander had not even been born. Thus, he was simply making an identification statement. The Colchians looked just like the Egyptians with their Black skin and wooly hair. It was plain to him that Egypt was different geographically from other nations such as Greece and Persia.

Herodotus recounts a conversation that carried on between Greeks about women who were foreigners. At first it seemed that the women spoke like doves, that is, birds, to the Greeks, then when one of the women learned the Greek language, the Greeks said that the women now spoke like human beings. The Greeks referred to the doves as Black to indicate that they were Egyptians. Herodotus says that the account he heard was that "two Black doves flew away from Egyptian Thebes and while one directed its flight to Libya, the other came to them. She alighted on an oak, and sitting there began to speak with a human voice" (Herodotus, Book II, 57).

Furthermore, he writes: "The Dodonaeans called the women doves because they were foreigners, and seemed to them to make a noise like birds." He then says, "...by calling the dove Black the Dodonaeans indicated that the woman was an Egyptian" (Herodotus, *Book II*, 57).

The Study of Ancient Egypt

Ancient Egypt refers to Archaic and Pharaonic Egypt. The critics of Afrocentricity make two main arguments against the study of ancient Egypt. First, they say that Afrocentrists are not interested in other parts of Africa, and secondly, that Afrocentrists are interested in replicating the Greek model in Egypt. But these are inaccurate statements that have little basis in fact. More significantly theoretically however is the fact that both objections stem from a White supremacist location and illustrates precisely the false intellectual line that Afrocentrists have uncovered. To say that the Afrocentrists are not interested in other parts of Africa is patently unsupportable. But what the objection to the study of Egypt reveals is the resurgence of the 19th century idea of a "True Negro" now metamorphosed as a "true Africa." What this objection to Egypt as Africa shows is the continuing difficulty Europeans have dealing with Africa, the most diverse continent on the face of the earth as far as human DNA is concerned.

Most Afrocentrists have a transcontinental African consciousness about research so the entire African world and all of its phenomena and penumbrations are open to this dynamic historiography. Scholars are eager to engage African in ways that suggest agency and centrality, that is, Africa as subject and actor in its own sphere and the world. New discoveries made by Afrocentrists and non-Afrocentrists in Ghana, Nigeria, Benin, Cameroon, South Africa, Malagasy are just as interesting as those made in Egypt and Nubia. But why should we leave out the study of Egypt?

"Locating the Eurocentric Assumptions about African History"
Molefi Kete Asante
Temple University

Should Afrocentrists abandon their interest in Algeria and Morocco before Islam? Shall we not encourage our students to conceive a history of Africa written from an African point of view? The meaning of such a point of view is, of course, Afrocentric.

The second objection to our study of Egypt is that we have been boxed into a reactive position of trying to study Egypt as a counter to Greece. This complaint is baseless and probably derives from a misunderstanding of Cheikh Anta Diop's dictum that "Egypt is to Africa as Greece is to Europe" (Diop, 1977). He believed that a history of Africa could not be written without including the Nile Valley civilizations. It would be like writing about Asia without China and India or Europe without Greece and Rome. The belief that he was encouraging a history of monuments is incorrect but even had he sought to make such a suggestion it would be false to see it as a response to Greece. After all, Egypt predates Greece and if anything Greece is a response to Egypt and the Greek scholars are nothing more than interpreters of an imitative society. But we all know history is far subtler than this harsh judgment. People tend to study what is accessible in terms of evidence, documents, and artifacts. Egypt possesses more historical documents than any other African civilization, perhaps more than any civilization in terms of the first and second millennia before Christ. It is therefore quite normal for more scholars to be interested in this locality.

Evidentiary records of such a society are largely of the official sort. Since we have an abundance of ready sources scholars cannot ignore them precisely because they are official. One always seeks to uncover the "real deal" and sometimes the official documents give enough evidence to assist in deeper analysis of the lives of ordinary people. Nevertheless the insistence that when Afrocentrists study Egyptians' official documents this is somehow a concern with replicating the Greek model of monument and is another example of a poor understanding of the Afrocentric objective. Casting Greece or what Europeans writers have done as the categorical standard is assuming a pre-eminence in interpretation and history that has neither been properly earned nor is rightly deserved given the numerous self serving and racist explanations of ancient history that one finds in Eurocentric histories.

Kemet as an Example

The ancient Egyptian word "kmt" or "Kemet" has been arbitrarily interpreted by Eurocentric scholars to mean "the Black Land." They say that the word "kmt" could not have meant "Black People" or "Black Nation" because the Egyptians were making a comment about the Blackness of the soil. The ground was Black, they say. The only reason many of the early European Egyptologists could not see the meaning of "kmt" was because they refused to believe that the people were describing themselves and their nation. Or more criminally they took the chance of shifting the meaning of the word to effect a grand conspiracy against the ancient Africans. I am more inclined to believe the first reason. The word "kmt" means literally "The Black Nation" or "The Black City." To arrive at any other conclusion one must make all kinds of unreasonable mental contortions.

Although the determinative that refers to a place named, the niswet, occurs in most instances where the word appears, many scholars have been reluctant to let go of the idea that the word "kmt" meant Black dirt. They look the facts in the face and experience cognitive dissonance. After all, African, to them, was outside of history and clearly the Egyptians could not have been describing their land by reference to themselves. We can see how foolish this line of reasoning is by appealing to the language itself.

Some writers argue that "kmt" but be seen in the light of "dsrt" where one is "Black land" and the other is "red land." But there is no uniformly Black land in Egypt. At the Delta one could find silt from the inundation but this would be no different from silt from floods in other countries. Indeed, near Heliopolis, Ionuwu, we find some of the most dramatically red soil. One would have

"Locating the Eurocentric Assumptions about African History"
Molefi Kete Asante
Temple University

to argue unconvincingly that Heliopolis was not ever a part of this Black land if one held to the theory of Black soil. In the ancient Egyptian language the red land is more often written as hill country rather than with the determinative for city, niswet.

The impact of the Afrocentric idea is seen in the new interpretation of "kmt." European scholars are now admitting that the explanation for the glyphs cannot be "Black soil." They have come to this understanding since African scholars have been making serious study of the Mdw Ntr. Now that reasonable scholars concede the point, made so emphatic by the ancients use of the niswet as a determinative, that "kmt" means "Black country" or "Black nation" what does it mean? In the first place the evidence is overwhelming that the main determinative refers to an organized political unit, a city, province, or country. Although some Whites refer to "kmt" as the "Black city" we must insist that this is a unique determinative understood to represent the name of the country much like one would say Finns Land, Finland, Zulus Land, Zululand, Hun Land, Hungaria, or Angles Land, England.

There is an archaic interpretation of "kmt" and a more modern one. Both have speculative power but only one can be said to have the authority of historical and linguistic evidence. "Kmt" in the archaic interpretation, as I am using the term, meant for the European scholars "Black soil" as I have indicated. But now in a more modern sense they have revised the text to say that it means "Black city." There is an acceptance of the Afrocentrists' contention that niswet, as a determinative, indicates a political entity. Admission that "kmt" means, "Black city" presents other problems for the Eurocentric writers. If it now means, "Black city" why would the Egyptians use color to describe a city? There is no "brown city" or "White city" or "red city." If "kmt" is now "Black city" in the text of the modern Egyptologists then it cannot mean "Black dirt" or "Black soil." The word "Black", "km" did not carry negative connotations as it has in many modern European languages. To speak of Egypt as "Kmt" was to speak of a country not of dirt. Even

those who argue for the connection between "dsrt" are intellectually imperiled because they cannot discover the parallel that supposedly existed in the past, that is, in the minds of the early
Egyptologists, between "The Black Land" and "The Red Land."
They are not parallel because they are not in the same genre of
place. The desert could not be said to exist in the North of the
country and "Kmt" in the South when the desert actually existed
everywhere, south to north, that was not alongside the Nile River.

A Discourse of Dishonesty

This entire linguistic enterprise seemed to be constructed for
one reason: to deny that the ancient Egyptians were Black skinned
people. The exasperation White scholars of the last generation
and their descendants have demonstrated about assigning the
achievements of the African nation of Egypt to Black people
clearly illustrates the racial bias in historical analysis. Why would
every Egyptologist open his book with a description of Egypt that
said in effect that the people of Africa who created the pyramids
and the marvelous civilization along the Nile Valley were not
Black? There is only one reason for this defensive position and
that is to disconnect Egypt from the rest of Africa. In no other
example of ancient history can we find a similar response to the
material culture of the people. There is no debate about who built
the Great Wall of China or who built the Parthenon. No contest
over the ethnicity or racial classification of an ancient people has
ever reached the level of the discourse on Egypt. Fed by the desire
to defend the primacy and supremacy of the White race, Egyptologists sold their intellectual rights to those who paid their bills.

J. Gardner Wilkinson's *The Ancient Egyptians*, was an influential work first published in 1836, a few years after Champollion's
deciphering of the Mdw Ntr, and re-issued as recent as 1994.
Wilkinson wrote that the Egyptians were "undoubtedly from Asia;
as is proved by the form of the skull, which is that of a Caucasian
race, by their features, hair, and other evidences; and the whole

valley of the Nile throughout Ethiopia, all Abyssinia, and the coast to the south, were peopled by Asiatic immigrations" (Wilkinson, 1994). In an extended discussion of the origin of these creators of the ancient monuments along the Nile, Wilkinson goes on to explain that "The Egyptians probably came to the Valley of the Nile as conquerors. Their advance was through Lower Egypt southwards; and the extraordinary notion that they descended, and derived their civilization from Ethiopia has long since been exploded" (Wilkinson, 1994).

While it is true that no serious scholar would write a description such as this today the descendants of Wilkinson are found everywhere in the Academy. Arthur Schlesinger, Jr. used a quote from a letter to him by Miriam Lichtheim to defend his position that the ancient Egyptians were not Black people. Lichtheim, according to Schlesinger, went so far as to say: "The Egyptians were not Nubians, and the original Nubians were not Black. Nubia gradually became Black because Black peoples migrated northward out of Central Africa" (Schlesinger, 1992).

The position advanced by Wilkinson became the reigning opinion of White scholars for more than a century and his influence continues until today. Of course, Wilkinson, even in 1836, could have had better authority than he took advantage of to write his section on the race and origin of the Egyptians. Other observers, some much earlier, had already made more insightful commentaries about the ancient Egyptians. Count Constantin de Volney had written as early as 1791 in his book *The Ruins: or a Survey of the Revolution of Empires* exclaimed, "How are we astonished...when we reflect that to the race of Negroes at present our slaves, and the objects of our extreme contempt, we owe our arts, sciences, and even the very use of speech; and when we recollect that, in the midst of those nations who call themselves the friends of liberty and humanity, the most barbarous of slaveries is justified, and that it is even a problem whether the understanding of Negroes be of the same species with that of White men!" (1791).

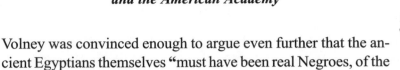
Volney was convinced enough to argue even further that the ancient Egyptians themselves "must have been real Negroes, of the same species with all the natives of Africa" (Volney, 1783).

Other European scholars went against the leading edge of White supremacist teachings to announce the obvious. For example, the German scholar Erman wrote in 1866: "Nothing exists in the physical structure of the ancient Egyptian to distinguish him from the native African" (Erman, 1971). Neither Volney nor Erman were to convince enough of their European fellows that their observations were valid and therefore as late as 1971 we find Egyptologists of the old school appearing in the words of David O'Connor who writes that "Thousands of sculpted and painted representations from Egypt and hundreds of well-preserved bodies from its cemeteries show that the typical physical type was neither Negroid nor Negro" (Anthropology, 1971).

O'Connor was just following the line laid down by earlier writers such as Wilkinson and Maspero. Indeed in *Histoire ancienne des peuples de l'Orient* Maspero had declared "On examining innumerable reproductions of statues and bas-reliefs, we recognized at once that the people represented on the monuments instead of presenting peculiarities and the general appearance of the Negro, really resembled the fine White races of Europe and Western Asia (Maspero, 1917).

Maspero was clearly playing to those in whose service he was and cannot be considered serious in this observation or another one where he claims that the Egyptians "were Black skinned Whites!" We are here in the terrain of the mystical.

Fortunately for us we have science as a guide in our analysis and synthesis of phenomena. In this way Afrocentrists have been able to confront the arguments advanced against an African point-of-view, pointing out that most of the time the attacks have not been based on a close location of the issues but rather the anticipated response of those who feel that their prerogatives are threatened. Hopefully, we are on the road to a more authoritative pluralism.

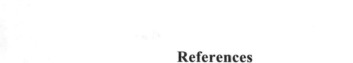

References

"Ancient Egypt and Black Africa: Early Contacts," *Expedition: The Magazine of Archaeology/Anthropology*, 14, 1971, p. 2.

Aristotle, *Physiognomonica*.

Molefi Kete Asante, *The Afrocentric Idea*. Philadelphia: Temple University Press, 1999.

Molefi Kete Asante, "The Ideology of White Supremacy and the European Slave Trade," paper presented at UNESCO Conference on "The Slave Routes" in Lisbon, Portugal, December, 1998.

Katherine Bankole, *Slavery and Medicine*. New York: Garland Press, 1997.

Black Issues in Higher Education, May, 1996.

Cheikh Anta Diop, *Parente genetique de l'Egyptien Pharaonique et des langues Negro-Africaine*. Dakar: IFAN, Les Nouvelles Editions Africaines, 1977, p. xxv.

Adolf Erman, *Life in Ancient Egypt*. New York: Dover Publications, 1971 (originally published in 1886 in German and in English in 1894), p. 29.

J. D. Fage, *A History of West Africa*. London: Oxford University Press, 1969, pp. 2-14.

Georg Hegel, *Reason in History*. Trans. R. Hortman. Indianapolis: Bobbs-Merrill, 1982, p. 3; W. Breasted, *Development of Religion and Thought in Ancient Egypt*. 1911; and Gaston Maspero, *Histoire ancienne des peuples de l'Orien*. Paris: Hachette, 1917, pp. 17-18.

Herodotus, Histories, *Book II*, 55

Herodotus, Histories, *Book II*, 57

Herodotus, Histories, *Book II*, 57

Arthur Schlesinger, Jr., *The Disuniting of America*. Knoxville: Whittle Communications, 1992, p. 130.

Audrey Smedley, *Race in North America: The Origin and Evolution of a Worldview*. Boulder, Colo.: Westview Press, 1998, 2nd Ed., pp. 23-26.

Arnold Toynbee, *A Study of History*. London: Oxford University Press, 1987, Volume One, pp. 5-23.

C. F. Volney, *The Ruins: Or a Survey of the Revolution of Empires*. London: G.G.J. and James Robinson, 1791.

C. F. Volney, *Travels Through Syria and Egypt in the Years 1783, 1784, and 1785*. London: G.G.J. and James Robinson, 1787.

J. Gardner Wilkinson, *The Ancient Egyptians*. London: Guernsey, 1994, p. 302.

Wilkinson, p. 303.

Gaston Maspero, *Histoire ancienne des peuples de l'Orien*. Paris: Hachette, 1917, pp. 17-18, 12th ed., translated as *The Dawn of Civilization*. London, 1894, and reprinted by Frederick Ungar, New York, 1968.

Toward an African Historiography
Jacob Gordon
University of Kansas

Although the study of African history in the historical profession is a recent development, the writing of African history is as old as history itself. In writing about the development of African historiography the British historian, J.D. Fage (1969) reviewed several works by early historians of Africa. Although he had serious problems in his conceptualization of African history, Fage was astute enough to note that historians of the ancient Mediterranean world and those of medieval Islamic civilization both took the whole known worlds as their frame of reference. Indeed Fage suggested that North African history continued to be part of the mainstream of western historical studies until the advance of the Ottoman Turkish Empire in the sixteenth century.

African historians had long been unknown to the West although the West had written about Africa. One such major African historian was Ibn Khaldun (1332-1406), who, because of his extensive writings about Africa must be called the "Father of African History." Ibn Khaldun was a North African, a native of Tunis. Other works of this period include Leo Africanus', *A Geographical History of Africa, Pliny's Natural History*, and the writings of such Arab scholars as Mas'udi (c.950); al-Bakri (1029-94); al-Idrisi (1154); Yukut (c. 1200); Abu al-Fida (1273-1331); al-Umari (1301-49); Ibn Battuta (1304-69). Thus for the most part African history has been written in Arabic and European languages, indicating the dominance of those cultures in African political, social, and religious life during an anemic period of African history.

Indigenous African languages such as Hausa, Serere, Wolof, Lingala, Akan, Edo, Igbo, Juri, Yoruba and Swahili have been neglected in African historiography. African historians have not

25

resorted to the use of African languages as much as they should have in the creation of a historiography. Most African historians still write in non-African languages. Moreover, much of African history remains as an appendage to Arabic or European history and historiography. However, it is Europe that has usurped the major role in the history of Africa in modern times.

European accounts of Africa continued for a long time to be the mainstream historical literature of Africa. Interesting examples of those studies include Richard Burton's (1821-90) *Travels in Africa* in the nineteenth-century; A.P. Newton's lectures to the Royal African Society in London on "Africa and Historical Research" in which he asserted that "Africa had no history before the coming of the Europeans." Furthermore, there were other works in the same vein. Works by James Steven (1789-1859) and Herman Merivale (1806-74) attempted to place Africa within a historical context understandable to Europeans. However, the larger works, comprehensive in nature, that dealt with Africa always seem to analyze Africa as the categorical inferior. One could simply see the works of Arnold Toynbee, the *New Cambridge Modern History*; the *Cambridge History of the British Empire* (1929-59); *Peuples et Civilisations, Histoire Generale*, 20 volumes, Paris, 1927-52; *Histoire Generale*, edited by G. Glotz, 10 volumes, Paris, 1925-38; *Propylaen Weltgeschichute in Banden* Bern, 1952; *Vsemirnaja Istorija* (World History), 10 volumes, Moscow, 1952.

More recent histories of Africa was written by professional colonial historians who were generally wedded to the concept that African people had no history, or no history that they could study or that was worth their studying (Fage, 1969). Much of these writings characterized the study of African history in the twentieth-century. However it should be noted that the Eurocentric approach to African history has not gone unchallenged. Such scholars as Cheikh Anta Diop, Molefi Asante, Chinweizu, Ayi

"Toward an African Historiography"
Jacob Gordon
University of Kansas

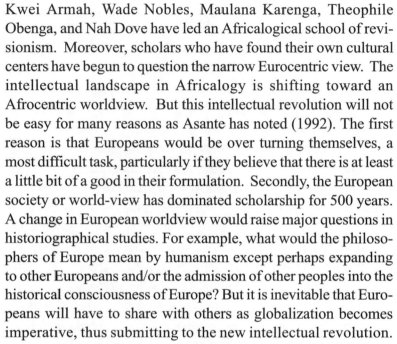

Kwei Armah, Wade Nobles, Maulana Karenga, Theophile Obenga, and Nah Dove have led an Africalogical school of revisionism. Moreover, scholars who have found their own cultural centers have begun to question the narrow Eurocentric view. The intellectual landscape in Africalogy is shifting toward an Afrocentric worldview. But this intellectual revolution will not be easy for many reasons as Asante has noted (1992). The first reason is that Europeans would be over turning themselves, a most difficult task, particularly if they believe that there is at least a little bit of a good in their formulation. Secondly, the European society or world-view has dominated scholarship for 500 years. A change in European worldview would raise major questions in historiographical studies. For example, what would the philosophers of Europe mean by humanism except perhaps expanding to other Europeans and/or the admission of other peoples into the historical consciousness of Europe? But it is inevitable that Europeans will have to share with others as globalization becomes imperative, thus submitting to the new intellectual revolution.

A major challenge for the writing of African history in the 21st century and in the new millennium is to reverse this trend. This charge requires a new historiography of Africa and a redefinition of the study of Africa. Thus this paper examines five related African history content areas for conceptualizing a new African historiography that is comprehensive, universal and scientific. Indeed the work of the principal Afrocentric scholars must be seen in the light of these five related African history content areas for conceptualization of a new historiography. Inasmuch as historians have not actually re-conceptualized the way they have written history it remains a task that must be done by Afrocentric historians.

African History in the African Context

The place of history in African society is important. African history must be viewed within the context of the African environ-

27

ment as a part of the human experience. Other integral points of the African context include African value systems, kinship systems, economic attitudes, religious views and philosophical aspects of ordinary life. All of these constituents of the African context beg to be examined from an Afrocentric worldview.

Africans like other human beings on earth are products of the environment. Geography is the handmaiden of history. Indeed the history of humanity has always shown the deep mark of environment. In other words, the development of humankind can be seen as a struggle for freedom from the limitations of the surroundings, as an effort to control environment rather than suffer its restraints. Thus to understand the great historical movements in Africa, it is not only necessary but imperative to grasp the essentials of Africa's geography, its physical features, vegetation, and rainfall. These factors have direct impact on African history. For example, the geographic base of Africa provides a background for understanding the genesis of humankind and the origins of agriculture in Africa as well as the rise and fall of African kingdoms, the world of the desert and African trade with the outside world. It is important to note that most of Africa is within the tropics, that is Africa's equatorial location, its northern and southern extremes almost equidistant from the equator at 37° 21' north and 34° 51' south respectively. Of an estimated size of 12 million square miles, more than nine million square miles of Africa, or four-fifths of its area, lie between the two tropics of Cancer and Capricorn. Thus it is clear that Africa's geographical location has a great impact on African way of life, hence African history.

The "Great Migrations" in African civilization have had a tremendous impact in African history. According to Olaniyan, (1982), the study of African migration makes it possible to address the vital questions of how different African societies came to be where they are; how cultures, civilizations and states evolved;

and to what extent external influences or internal forces can be used to explain the growth of African cultures. It is important to note that prehistoric peoples in Africa were nomadic, hunter-gatherers, uninhibited by pressure of population, were free to move where game and wild foods were plentiful. The material culture of these early societies was of necessity simply as was their social organization; they existed in an intimate, precarious balance with nature and their environment. Other important considerations include the domestication of plants and animals, the development of agriculture and the introduction and spread of iron technology, trade and most importantly, the development of the states, especially the West African states, the Bantu Migration, and Bantu civilization. Equally important is the impact of migration on the growth of "stateless" societies in Africa.

African Value System and Worldview

It is generally accepted that all human behaviors are driven by culture. Indeed the significance of events is derived from human cultures. Thus it can be concluded that all events of large significance take place within the setting of some culture. African value systems are culturally based or guided by African cultures. African cultures are defined in this context as African way of life, aesthetics, family values, and knowledge. Afrocentrically, a useful way to view African cultures lies in the understanding of culture as shared perceptions, attitudes, and predisposition that allow people to organize experiences in certain ways (Asante, 1990). According to Asante, the principal issues in Afrocentric inquiry are framed by cosmological, epistemological, axiological, and aesthetic considerations. In this regard, Asante agrees that the Afrocentric method pursues a world voice distinctly African-centered in relationship to external phenomena.

Essential to any serious research in African studies is a consideration of the cosmos. Epistemologically, the search for the

truth must reflect the African reality including its ancestral memo-
ries and languages. The axiological perspectives raise the question of values. This is at the core of African cultures especially
the African family value system. What, for example, constitutes
good and bad, right and wrong?

African Religion and Philosophy

The development of African religion and philosophy predates
the coming of Christianity and Islam. African historiography cannot abandon the role of traditional ideas and religion in Africa
before alien intrusion into African civilization. Equally important is the impact of alien religions and ideas to Africa. To ignore
one in favor of the other is to create an omission and distortion in
African history. In addressing this subject, Mbiti has empha-
sized the unity of African religious and philosophy in order to
give an overall picture of their situation. The obvious weakness
in this approach is that it does not give room for the treatment in
depth of individual religious and philosophical systems of different African peoples.

However, religious practices from all over the continent were
used in the book by John Mbiti. He made general observations
and gave detailed illustrations. It was not until the 1960s that the
rest of the world, except Africa, began to take African religions
and philosophy seriously. Throughout the 19th century and more
than half of the 20th century, African religions and philosophy
were viewed from Eurocentric anthropological perspectives. An
important component of African religion and philosophy for conceptualizing African historiography is its supernatural aspect.

African History and the Islamic Tradition

A neglected aspect of African history and historiographical
methods is the Arabic tradition and Islamic impact on Africa. Some
of the earliest works on Africa were done by Arab scholars – the

ulamas in the Arabic language. Islam is doctrinally concerned with ultimate causation, truth and morality, and with humans relation to their Creator. It has a code of ethics, set of beliefs and a way of life.

Historically, the Arabs and their religion of Islam reached Africa in the 7th century AD. Between the death of Islam's founder, Mohammad, in A.D. 632 and the middle of the eighth century, the Arabs carried the new faith to all parts of the Asia, the Mediterranean, central and western Asia, and North Africa. In their wake they left a new civilization proposing a new universalism and based on their own language and means of writing. Within a short time the rest of Africa was opened to Islamic religions and economic penetration. For example, by the 18th century, local histories in the Arabic script were produced in many parts of Africa, including the greater Islamic center like Timbuktu or Kano. These events undoubtedly impacted African history and culture. They must equally be important factors in African historiography.

African History and the African Diaspora

The interest of peoples of African descent in African history has been well documented. Most notable among the pioneer works were George Washington William's *History of the Negro Race in America from 1619 to 1880* in 1882; W.E.B. Du Bois' classic doctoral dissertation at Harvard University. "The Suppression of the African Slave Trade to the United States of America, 1638-1870," in 1895, and Carter G. Woodson's establishment of the Association for the Study of African-American Life and History (ASALH) in 1915-16. Other Diasporan major contributors include the works of Edward Blyden, George Padmore, C.L.R. James, Eric Williams, John Hope Franklin, Chancellor Williams, Alex Haley, and Price Mars. Undoubtedly, Woodson's academic entrepreneurship laid the foundation for Black history in America as a specialty in the historical profession (Meier and Rudwick, 1986).

The development of African Studies on American college campuses in the late 1950's and 60's was for the most part the product of Black American student movement. It was a part of the Black student's demand for the inclusion of the African and the African Diasporan dimensions in the curriculum and extra-curricular activities of American colleges and universities. The responses to this demand were overwhelming in the late 60's as European-Americans joined Black students in questioning the legitimacy and relevance of American higher educational institutions. By the 1970's most major colleges and universities had created Black studies, African studies and/or Caribbean studies programs. San Francisco State, UCLA, Cornell, Northwestern, Michigan State and Howard led the way. Today many universities now offer advanced degrees in African and/or African Diaspora studies. These include Harvard University, Temple University, Indiana University, The University of Kansas, and Yale University.

Likewise, several academic and professional organizations have been established since 1915 when Woodson founded the Association for the Study of African American Life and History. These include African Studies Association (ASA) the largest of all; Southern Conference on Afro-American Studies (SCASSI); National Association of African American Studies (NAAAS); National Council of Black Studies (NCBS). The ASA is predominately White although in recent years African and African American scholars have played a major role in its leadership. The various activities of these professional organizations and the thousands of published research materials by scholars including books, monographs, articles and research reports have helped to shape the study of African history and must therefore be of some consideration in conceptualizing African historiography. Africa as seen by peoples of the African descent in the new world is an academic and social dimension that the historiography of Africa cannot ignore (Keita, 2000).

African History and the West

Throughout the 19th and most of the 20th centuries, African history and African Historiography, were dominated by the Western worldview. In the same way Western historiography was dominated by the European philosophers and historians. The general view of European historians, beginning in the 14th century, was that the only history that was of any significance was the study of "western civilization," from its origin in ancient Greece, Rome, and Judea (Fage, 1969). By the end of the 18th century, this culture had become possessed of technological and economic strengths that enabled it to dominate the rest of the world. European historians paid no attention to earlier great civilizations in Africa and Asia nor did they recognize some of the major roles of Africans in the Greco-Roman Empire (Snowden, 1970). In his 1828 lecture on the philosophy of history, Hegel advanced the view that Africa " is no historical part of the world: it has no movement or development to exhibit"(Hegel, 1956).

Until very recently European historians gave scant attention to the culture and history of parts of the world outside Europe, whose people they thought had made no contributions to the general progress of humankind. Thus there was no treatment of Africa whatsoever in the first *Cambridge Modern History*. This publication was, Fage pointed out, a great cooperative work, which marked a high point of historical learning at the beginning of the 20th century. In his famous work, "A Study of History," Arnold Toynbee wrote, "History begins when men take to writing." Another distinguished British scholar, Professor A.P. Newton, said, "Africa had no history before it was colonized by Europeans." These historians disregarded the African origin of human

33

civilization; indeed, they tried to disregard the African origin of the human race. Civilizations of the Nile Valley, such as the Badari, Kemetic, and Meroitic were simply dismissed as non-African although they were in Africa or ignored altogether. There were still other western historians who maintained, either that such histories could not be properly studied, or that they were not worth studying. Among these was the Regius Chair of Modern History in the University of Oxford, Professor Hugh Trevor-Roger, who is said to have made the unkind remark that what had happened in Africa was no more than the "unrewarding gyrations of barbarous tribes."

European historians generally discredited such African history as was written by the 19th century precursors of Pan-Africanism, such as Edward W. Blyden, the 19th century Ghanaian cleric, Carl Christian Reindorf, or the Yoruba historian, Samuel Johnson, or the work of Joseph Isharam of Benin. These works and several others were regarded by European historians as the works of gifted and dedicated amateurs who were not recognized by the professional historians and whose work was little regarded in the universities and in schools. This attitude is either a reflection of Western arrogance of racial superiority and/or ignorance.

Since 1947 however, there has been a revolution in African historiography. That year marked the effective beginning of the modern movement which has led to the establishment of the University of Ibadan in Nigeria and the University of Ghana in 1948 and other institutions of higher learning throughout tropical Africa. It is also important to note here that during this period Western historians were forced from their position of denial of the existence of African history to the acknowledgment of African history from European perspectives. The works of colonial administrators, travelers and missionaries shaped western historians' view of Africa. Thus the colonization of African history as an appendage to European history was *a fait accompli*. But the new African universities had the blessings of Africans who had gone abroad to study in the United States, Great Britain, France, and other European countries and the non-western nations like the Caribbean. These scholars and African nationalists like Kwame Nkrumah, Nnamdi Azikiwe, Jomo Kenyatta, and Julius Nyerere began to challenge western perceptions of African and African history. Although the resolution toward the reconstruction of African history has met with some successes, the movement continues to labor under the influence of a myth of White superiority.

References

Molefi Kete Asante, *Kemet, Afrocentricity and Knowledge*. Trenton: Africa World Press, 1990.

J. D. Fage, *A History of West Africa*. London: Oxford University Press, 1969.

Georg Hegel, *Lectures on the Philosophy of World History*. Tr. J. Sibree. New York: Dover, 1956.

Maghan Keita, *Race and the Writing of History: Riddling the Sphinx*. New York: Oxford University Press, 2000.

Critiquing the Critics: Advancing the Paradigm
Charles Finch, III
Morehouse College

In the fall of 1989, I participated in a symposium convened by Professor Molefi Asante at Temple University where a varied group of scholars were invited to discuss and debate the merits of Martin Bernal's *Black Athena*. The paper I delivered, entitled *The African Sources of Greek Myths,* opened as follows: "In historical times, the world has probably never seen the emergence of a 'single-source' culture." That statement is as applicable now as ever and *particularly* applies to ancient Greece. To paraphrase Asa Hilliard, ancient Greek civilization was not the product of a cultural "immaculate conception." It is a chimerical idea and, as a paradigm of history, first appeared about 200 years ago as an outgrowth of an interpretative movement among German antiquarians that Martin Bernal has dubbed the "Aryan Model." Down to the Common Era, one can search the ancient literature virtually in vain for any hint of a suggestion that the civilization of the Greeks, proud as they were of it, had emerged fully formed, *sui generis,* and free of influences from surrounding cultures.

Modern classicists find themselves in an incongruous position: their unbounded admiration for all that Greek thinkers achieved in philosophy, mathematics, astronomy, music, the plastic arts—indeed all of the humanities, liberal arts and sciences—is matched only by their smug condescension toward the putative Greek credulity and naiveté when writing about their own history. Many classicists take the position, clearly exemplified in the book by Mary Lefkowitz, *Not Out of Africa,* that they know more about the "true" history of the ancient Greeks than the Greeks themselves, a bizarre claim made also by not-a-few antiquarian scholars in other fields. With some rare and notable exceptions, European antiquarian scholars tend to act as if the ancients were not qualified to write about their own history to the same degree as people living several thousand years after them. Classicists seem to want it both ways: they want to pontificate about the great accomplishments of civilizations they claim are ancestral to themselves but to ignore the profound debt these same civilizations owed to other high cultures, especially African ones.

Northeast Africa, i.e., the Nile Valley, played as formative a role in the early evolution of Greek culture as Greece did Western civilization. Everything proclaims it, including all the ancient Greek commentators who mentioned the subject. At present, it is possible to travel to any corner of the globe and find cassette tapes by Michael Jackson, Madonna, and Tupac Shakur, powerful testimony to the extraordinary global influence of American popular culture. Nile Valley civilization exercised a similar influence over all of the civilized Old World west of the Indus. Nile Valley high culture is already complete and mature by 4,000 B.C. and remained an intact and powerful force for the next four millennia. Over large swaths of that time, Egypt was the political overlord of most of the eastern half of the Mediterranean and even when not in political control, her cultural hegemony was paramount. She left her imprint everywhere, not only in material artifacts, but also in customs, practices, beliefs, and rituals. It is not strange that we should find a pronounced Nilotic influence on the northern Mediterranean nations of antiquity, it would be strange if we did not.

Architecture

In architecture, Egypt is the first to raise massively precise edifices in stone, elaborating architectural styles whose influence would eventually even be felt as far away as Mexico. The so-called "Doric column" had already achieved a perfection of form by the 3rd Dynasty, more than 3,000 years before the building of the Parthenon. No other culture would build so widely, massively and prolifically in stone. Even the original Temple at Jerusalem, erected by Solomon, was "built on the ground plan of an Egyptian temple" according to James Henry Breasted.

Sculpture

In sculpture and statuary, Egypt set standards that have lasted for all time. The sphinx-form spread itself over the entire civilized world west of India. The Egyptian canon of proportion—one that often incorporated the Golden Number—became the standard measure of beauty and harmony in sculpture. The Greeks of 6th century—in the fashion of apprentices—sculpted careful imitations of Egyptian statues now known as *Kouros* statues. Thus, the first artistically important sculptures of post-Mycenaean Greece owed as much to the Egyptian form as Michelangelo's *Pieta* or *David* owed to his ancient Greek predecessors.

Astronomy

In astronomy, almost every Greek writer who mentions the subject traces the origin of scientific astronomy to Egypt and Chaldea, though always giving priority to Egypt. Testaments to the Nilotic proficiency in astronomy abound. They developed no fewer than three calendars: lunar, Sirian-solar, and precessional. The precessional calendar is derived from the retrograde movement of the celestial North Pole around the ecliptic North Pole, encompassing a period of 26,000 years. The Sirian solar calendar is based on the difference between the true year of 365 days determined by the heliacal rising of the Sirius at the summer solstice and the civil calendar conventionalized at 365 days. With the civil calendar slipping back relative to the Sirian 1~ day every year, it took 1460 years for the two calendars to re-synchronize. In late antiquity, at the insistence of first the Ptolemies, then Julius Caesar, the calendrists of Kemet devised a leap year to reconcile the two calendars.

Systematic stargazing had been going on in the Nile Valley long before the beginning of the dynastic period around 4,000

B.C. Moreover, there are records of Nile Valley astronomers predicting lunar eclipses going back to middle of the 8th century B.C. They were among the earliest, as the Greeks said, to identify the constellations that Thales brought from the Nile to Greece. These astronomer-priests were also the first to devise the 24-hour day.

Mathematics

It is again to the Nile Valley that we must look for evidence of the early influence on Greek mathematics. With respect to geometry, the commentators are unanimous: the mathematician-priests of Nile Valley knew no peer. The geometry of Pythagoras, Eudoxus, Plato, and Euclid was learned in Nile Valley temples. Four mathematical papyri still survive, most importantly the Rhind mathematical papyrus dating to 1832 B.C. Not only do these papyri show that the priests had mastered all the processes of arithmetic, including a theory of number, but had developed formulas enabling them to find solutions of problems with one and two unknowns, along with "think of a number problems." With all of this plus the arithmetic and geometric progressions they discovered, it is evident that by 1832 B.C., algebra was in place in the Nile Valley.

Problem No. 56 in the Rhind Papyrus gives an equation to find the angle of the slope of a pyramid's face, which in fact is its cotangent. With a cotangent, one automatically has a tangent by taking the inverse of the cotangent. Moreover, the means were present with pyramidal models to obtain sine and cosine values. Thus, trigonometry was also developed earliest in the Nile Valley. The advanced state of this math is confirmed by an architectural drawing even older than the Rhind Papyrus that shows that Nilotic engineers had learned to find the area under a curve more than 5,000 years ago. Finally, as Flinders Petrie found, the architects had several times built into their structures right triangles that obeyed the theorem: $a^2 + b^2 = c^2$~where a and b are the two

 40

sides and c is the hypotenuse. Since Pythagoras studied in the temples of the Nile Valley for 22 years it would not have surprised him to learn there was the source of the theorem that bears his name.

Medicine

Homer, in Book 4 of *The Odyssey* states simply, "in medicine, Egypt leaves the rest of the world behind." This quote and the many examples of foreign princes who retained Egyptian physicians testifies to their high repute and influence beyond their borders. The Persian emperors Cyrus and Darius each relied on an Egyptian personal physician. The medical papyri, particularly the Edwin Smith and the Ebers, supply ample evidence of the extraordinary skill of the ancient physicians of the Nile. These documents, whose originals date back to around 4,000 B.C., show a medical science already in full flower. The Edwin Smith shows a startling knowledge of neuroanatomy and neurophysiology, revealing 6000 years ago the ancient doctors' understanding of the relation between the temporal portion of the brain and language, speech, and hearing. *The Book of the Heart and Vessels*, a source book for both the Edwin Smith and the Ebers Papyri, shows that Nile Valley anatomo-physiologists had recognized the heart as the center of a circulatory system that sent blood through the major vessels emanating from it to the body's vital organs. Not surprisingly, Nile Valley physicians measured the pulse as an aid to diagnosis. Trephination, the forerunner of neurosurgery, was successfully performed in the Old Kingdom.

As to Hippocrates: he was unquestionably a physician of genius who is entirely deserving of his exalted 2500 year-old reputation. What he wasn't was the "Father of Medicine." He did not even compose the famed Hippocratic Oath. It is known that he was descended from a line of priests of Asclepios on the isle of Cos. By the 6th century B.C., Asclepios had become identified with the physician Imhotep who lived around 2,700 B.C.

and was called by Sir Williams Osler "the first figure of a physician to stand out clearly from the mists antiquity." It can be reasonably inferred that, like his forbears, Hippocrates revered Imhotep who, if anyone deserves the title "Father of Medicine," he does. From Alexandrian times (330 B.C. - 200 B.C.), the major medical figures of the Greco-Roman world studied in Egypt, including Galen, Herophilus, and Erasistratos. Egypt continued to "leave the rest of the world behind" in medical knowledge until well after the beginning of the Common Era.

Religion and Mythology

Herodotus and Diodorus are the two classical authorities that insist most strongly that Greece owed her rites, religion, and gods to Egypt and Ethiopia, i.e., Nile Valley civilization. Diodorus informs us that "the Ethiopians were the first to be taught to honor the gods and to hold sacrifices and festivals and processions...and other rites by which men honor the deity." Herodotus adds that "The names of nearly all the gods came to Greece from Egypt." He further asserts, "I will never admit that the similar ceremonies performed in Greece and Egypt are the result of mere coincidence—had that been so, our rites would have been *more Greek in character and less recent in origin.*"

Contrary to repeated assertions in *Not Out of Africa*, neither Diodorus nor Herodotus were uncritical Egyptophiles supinely accepting what the priests told them. Both of them were learned men, well read and well travelled. They crosschecked their information and consulted a variety of sources and informants, both Greek and Egyptian, then compared this information to their own personal observations. Their conclusions were carefully arrived at on the strength of a basically sound method of inquiry. Herodotus, in particular, was careful to differentiate between information and opinions drawn from others, his own observations, and his own interpretations. He was careful not to vouch for everything he heard but to record it as told for verification by others. That he was wrong on a number of points is more than compensated for by the independent corroboration of most of his account by later authorities, even up to the present.

The veneration and emulation of Nilotic religious practices begins with Homer (8th century B.C.) who in three places in The *Iliad* and *the Odyssey,* refers to the tendency of Olympian deities to go to feast among the blameless Ethiopians. Moreover, several other mythographers cite the African or Libyan provenance of important Olympians, demigods, heroes, and other Hellenic mythotypes. Dionysus and Athene were both born in Libya (Africa). Robert Graves says that the origins of Demeter are also to be looked for in Libya. Hercules, in one of his many guises, was said to have come from Egypt. A triad of Hellenic gods known to hail from Ethiopia was Helios, Eos, and Selene. Olympian deities not infrequently represented as Ethiopians—especially on the Kabeiric vases—were Aphrodite, Hera, and Artemis. Aphrodite was sometimes called *Melaenis,* i.e., "the Black One."

Certain mythological dramatis *personae* were distinctly Ethiopian in origin or depiction: Memnon, Tithonus, Cepheus, Cassiopeia, Andromeda, Theia (also *Melaena),* Delphos, Aeetes, Medea, Circe, Proteus, Phaeton, Eurybates, Danaus, Aegyptus, Belus, and Cephalus. What is more, there was sometimes such a close iden-tification between a Hellenic and an African god that the two be-came fused. Zeus, for example, was linked with the Nilotic Amon to such a degree that he became Zeus Ammon. It defies all evidence and logic to insist that Greek religion was not markedly impacted by Nile Valley religion. Religiously, we have as much evidence for a Nile-to-Greece link as we do for a Greece-to-Rome link.

Credibility Issues

A brief word about Greek sources and ancient historiography: if we accept Professor Lefkowitz's assertion that we cannot rely on the evidence put forward by an "over-credulous" group of ancient writers, then history itself must be jettisoned. The same method of attack can be applied to all historians of all times everywhere; it can be said that no historian's evidence is credible because he was moved by an implied emotion that compromises his conclusions. If we rely on this way of looking at it, history becomes impossible to write. Furthermore, Professor Lefkowitz "cross-examines her own witnesses," that is, discredits the very authorities that form the basis of the classical studies that constitute her whole career. This approach is not defensible; just because one does like the admiring manner in which Herodotus, Diodorus, Plato, Aristotle, and so many others speak about ancient African civilizations and acknowledge the Greek debt to them, doesn't mean that these savants didn't know what they were talking about.

As a new paradigm, evolving a new set of rules and premises, there are clearly occasions when the Afrocentric method can be questioned, particularly where the methodology lacks rigor. But *Not Out of Africa* does not show that the author is conversant with the whole range of the Afrocentric "school." She has read C.A. Diop, the "spiritual father" of Afrocentricity, but her criticisms of him are superficial and easily turned aside. She has not dealt with Theophile Obenga who has as comprehensive a command of Greco Roman antiquity as any person living, nor is she sufficiently conversant with the works of Ivan Van Sertima. Until the writings of Afrocentric scholars of this caliber are confronted and refuted, Afrocentricity, to paraphrase Molefi Asante, will stand as an authentic new paradigm not to be wished away by conservative academic opinion. Again, its manifesto is simply that where the history of people of African descent is concerned, Africa must sit at the center of its study.

Though scholars would vehemently deny it, myth-making either makes or rises out of history. Examples of national myths that decisively impacted the history of certain peoples include the "chosen people" mantle of the ancient Hebrews, the "manifest destiny" of an expansive American nation, and the "thousand-year Reich" of German National Socialism. If a people do not have a national myth, they create one because it is the myth that determines what they hope to be and what they strive for. Thus myths are not "fictions," they are the symbolic essence of a people's quest for meaning and destiny. It is too early to tell what, if any, enabling myth will rise out of the Afrocentric spirit. But the most conscientious of Afrocentric writers have no interest in fictions; we have spent too many years listening to those spun around our history by those who have sought to dominate us by controlling it.

The Power Of Myth: Dogon Philosophy

The myth, *so tame*, "astonishing word," which the Dogon consider to be "real" history, constitutes here the whole of coherent themes of creation; this is why, by virtue of their coherence and their order of succession, they make up a "history of the universe," aduno so *tame*. In the *Pale Fox* we learn that myth had to be understood not in an ordinary sense of an absurd poetic form, but as a master idea. It is a coherent system reserved for initiates who alone have access to deep knowledge.

Mythology

Just to indicate the extent of the relationship between the Egyptians and the Greeks I want to provide the following quotes as evidence of the close contact between the Greeks and the Africans. Indeed, the Greek writers attested to their relationships with the Africans. "Zeus made a twelve day journey to the shores of the ocean to feast among the blameless *Ethiopians"* (Homer, *The Iliad,* Book 1, lines 423-424). Furthermore, "...when they saw her (Iris), all the winds rose up with invitations....But she refused and said: I'm bound onward, across the streams of Ocean, to the *country of the Ethiopians;* hecatombs they'll make for the gods; *I* must attend the feast" (Homer, *The Iliad,* Book 23, lines 205-207).

Furthermore, "But now that god (Poseidon) had gone *far off among* the Ethiopians, most remote of men...in sunset lands and

45

the lands of the rising sun, to be regaled by smoke of thighbones burning, haunches of rams and bulls, a hundred fold. He lingered, delighted at the banquet table" (Homer, the *Odyssey,* Book 1, lines 25-31). Moreover, "the Ethiopians were the first to be taught to honor the gods and to hold sacrifices and festivals and processions and feasts and the other rites by which men honor the deity" according to Diodorus. Herodotus says that the priest told him "that the Egyptians first brought into use the names of the twelve gods, which the Greeks took over from them." He states further that "...it was not the Egyptians who took the name *Heracles* from the Greeks. The opposite is true: it was the Greeks who took it from the Egyptians..." –Herodotus, *Histories, Book II*.

It was clear that Herodotus understood the relationship between Egypt and Greece when he wrote that "Melampus ("Black-footed")...brought into Greece a number of things that he had learned in Egypt, and amongst them was the worship of Dionysus (Osiris). I will never admit that the similar ceremonies performed in Greece and Egypt are the result of mere coincidence—had that been so, our rites *would* have been more *Greek in* character and less recent in origin." –Herodotus, *Histories, Book II*. And finally, he tells his readers that "The names of nearly all the gods came to Greece from Egypt. I know *from* the *inquiries I have made* that they came from abroad, and it seems likely that it was from Egypt" –Herodotus, *Histories, Book II*.

Frank Snowden records in his book, *Blacks in Antiquity* that "The fifty sons of Aegyptus were described as Black....The Danaids described themselves as "Black and smitten by the sun"....To King Pelasgus they have the appearance of Libyans, or inhabitants of the Nille" (Snowden, p. 157). There is also the statement by Snowden that "Satyrs *(sileni* after *Silenus)* often resemble Negroes with respect to thickness of the lips and snubness of nose" (Snowden, p. 160). This has often led some people to assume that Socrates, who was described as a satyr or *silenus*, might have been African. We do not know this for a fact, only as a conjecture based on the meaning of the language.

Additional Linguistic and Historical Evidences

Robert Graves writes in his book *The Greek Myths* that "The castration of Uranus is not necessarily metaphorical if some of the victors *had originated in* East *Africa* where, to this day, the Galla warriors carry a miniature sickle into battle to castrate their enemies" (Graves, p. 38). Additionally, "According to the Pelasgians, the goddess Athene was born beside Lake Tritonis *in Libya...*" —Graves, quoting Apollonius Rhodius, p. 44. Again, "Plato identified Athene, patroness of Athens, with the Libyan goddess Neith..." —Graves, citing *Timaeus*.

In the book, *The Greek Myths*, Graves is sure that there is a connection between the Greek myths and Africa. He writes "...elsewhere [Aphrodite] was called Melaenis ("Black one")...[and]Scotia ("dark one")..." —(Graves, p. 72). "Demeter is said to have reached Greece by way of Crete....But Demeter's origin is to be looked for in Libya" —Graves, pp.95-96. "...the three Gorgons, dwellers in Libya" (Graves, p. 127). Furthermore, "When [Typhon] came rushing toward Olympus, the gods fled in terror to *Egypt* where they disguised themselves as animals: Zeus becoming a ram; Apollo a crow; Dionysus, a goat; Hera, a White cow; Artemis, a cat; Aphrodite, a fish; Ares, a boar; Hermes, an ibis, and so on"–(Graves, p. 134).

Of course it is clear that Herodotus was sure of what he saw and only reported what he saw or heard on good authority about the Blackness of the Egyptians. "At Dodona...the priestesses who deliver the oracles have a different version of the story: two Black doves, they say flew away from Thebes in Egypt, and one of them alighted at Dodona, and the other in Libya"-(Herodotus, *Histories, Book II*, p. 151). "As to the bird being Black [at Dodona], they merely signify by this that the woman was an

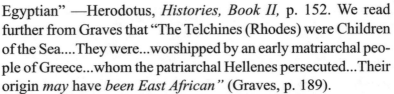
Egyptian" —Herodotus, *Histories, Book II,* p. 152. We read further from Graves that "The Telchines (Rhodes) were Children of the Sea....They were...worshipped by an early matriarchal people of Greece...whom the patriarchal Hellenes persecuted...Their origin *may* have *been East African"* (Graves, p. 189).

We know that Africa is all over the ancient Greek myths. Actually, we learn from Herodotus that "King Belus, who ruled Chemmis in Thebaid, was the son of Libya by Poseidon, and twin-brother of Agenor. His wife...daughter of Nilus, bore him the twins Aegyptus and Danaus and a third son Cepheus" (Graves, p. 200). We are told by the likes of Hyginus, Apollodorus, Herodotus, Strabo, Pausanias, and Plutarch that Danaus..had fifty daughters called the Danaids (born of Egyptian and Ethiopian mothers)....he built a ship for himself and his daughters...and sailed toward Greece together, by way of Rhodes....[He] became so powerful as a ruler that all the Pelasgians of Greece called themselves Danaans.

What's In A Name?

I have given a number of names below that have been researched and discovered by several scholars including Frank Snowden who wrote *Blacks in Antiquity.* This is not an exhaustive list but it is revealing. Greek and Roman Descriptions of Ethiopians or Blacks generally: aethiops, melas, melanochoros, niger, ater, aquilus, exustus, furvus, fuscus, and percotus. Additional Greco-Roman ethnonyms of Blacks: Afer (African), Indusllndi (India), Maurus (Moor). Greco-Roman toponyms of Africa—national, regional, continental:

Libya: derived from ancient Egyptian word *lebu,* given to the people who inhabited the lands west of the Nile.

India: in the ancient mind, Africa and continental India were linked; Indians were often called the *eastern Ethiopians*.

Ethiopia: An early Greek name, meaning "sunburnt," for the African countries and regions to the south and west of Egypt. The term *Ethiopia* was interchangeable with *Libya, India, Nubia,* and *Africa.*

Nubia: Latin term, derived from Egyptian word *nub* meaning "gold" referring to the southern fifth of Egypt plus the northern fifth of the Sudan.

Africa or *Afer:* Latin term, which came to be, and remains, the name for the entire continent.

Sources Of Greek Science

The biographies of Pythagoras are unanimous that at an early age he travelled widely to assimilate the wisdom of the ancients...He is said by Iamblichus to have spent some 22 years in Egypt studying there with the priests. —K.S. Guthrie, *the Pythagorean Source Book,* p. 20. Thales...advised him [Pythagoras] to go to Egypt, to get in touch with the priests of Memphis and Zeus. Thales confessed that the instruction of these priests *was the source of his own reputation for wisdom.* Guthrie, p. 59 (citing Iamblichus). He [Pythagoras] passed twenty-two years in the sanctuaries of temples, studying astronomy and geometry... —Guthrie/Iamblichus, p. 61. In Egypt he [Pythagoras] lived with the priests, and learned the language and the wisdom of the Egyptians, and their three kinds of letters, the epistolographic, the hieroglyphic, and symbolic... —Guthrie/ Porphyry, p. 125. In Egypt, Pythagoras had entered into the holiest parts of their temple, and learnt all the most secret mysteries that relate to their Gods. —Guthrie/Diogenes Laertius, p. 142.

Another influence [on Pythagoras] may have been Thales' belief that the universe began from water, an idea he *may* have

49

picked up from Egypt.-Peter Gorman, *Pythagoras: A Life, p.* 35. From this and the Egyptian hieratic myths concerning the creation of the world he [Thales] learned that the cosmos arose from the primeval water. —Gorman, p. 37. His [Pythagoras'] is such an important name in the history of philosophy that he actually invented the term "philosophy" or love of wisdom. —Gorman, p. 38. We now know that he might have in-vented it from the Egyptian word for wisdom, light, and truth, *Seba.* The symbolic method which Iamblichus claims Pythagoras learnt in Egypt was a system of presenting abstract truths in an enigmatic way. —Gorman, p. 80. Since the Greeks of his day *were not* educated in *the arcane* sciences *of Egypt and Babylon,* Pythagoras probably regarded them as children and sought to arouse their curiosity with riddles. —Gorman, p. 82. Clearly the evidence of Egyptian and Ethiopian influence and contact with the Greeks is overwhelming and no discussion of the ancient world is complete without a full discussion of these two African civilizations.

Lefkowitz and the Myth of the Immaculate Conception of Western Civilization:
The Myth is Not Out of Africa
Asa G. Hilliard, III
Fuller E. Callaway Professor
of Urban Education
Georgia State University

Think-tank slanting? Conservative think tanks behind a movement to curb the Food and Drug Administrations regulatory powers received at least $3.5 million from drug and tobacco companies over the past four years, according to a study by Public Citizen, a consumer watchdog group founded by Ralph Nadar. The seven think tanks have used the money to produce "a steady stream of reports, fact sheets, opinion page articles, and newspaper, radio and T.V. adds purporting to document the FDA's deadly overcaution and bullying of manufacturers," Public Citizen said. One of the think tanks, the American Enterprise Institute, called the report "diversionary." The report is to be released today. —The Atlanta Constitution, July, 24, 1996, p. A-3.

Mary Lefkowitz's book, *Not Out of Africa*, must be placed in context. A part of the context is the source of her sponsorship and her network and the nature of the public information effort of the network of which that sponsorship is a part. Is Mary Lefkowitz a part of a network that has a public policy and propaganda agenda? If so, *Not Out of Africa* must be read with that in mind.

The quotation above is but the tip of the iceberg of a growing awareness by some analysts of the role that privately-funded think tanks have played in shaping the images that Americans use to think about a variety of circumstances, including public policy, education and socialization.

David C. Berliner and Bruce J. Biddle have authored a brilliant analysis of what they call, *The Manufactured Crisis: Myths, Fraud*

 51

and the Attack on America's Public Schools (1995). The reactionary attack on schools shares with the attack on the regulation of the tobacco industry some of the same network of think tanks. Here is what Berliner and Biddle have to say about the motivations, identity and activity of this loose network. When explaining why the attack on public education has become so strident and severe in recent years, Berliner and Biddle have a chapter entitled, "Why Now?". Within that chapter, they answer that reactionary voices have been entitled.

Surely a major reason for increased criticism of schools in the 1980s was that reactionary voices were given more credence in America during that decade. When Americans elected Ronald Reagan, and afterwards George Bush, to the presidency, they made the expression of right-wing ideologues fashionable. Ideologues on the right had long been critical of the public schools, and once avowed conservatives were in the White House, those criticisms were granted legitimacy and given prominence by the press. This was, indeed, a break with recent history. . . . Early in the 1970s, however, a number of wealthy people with sharply reactionary ideas began to work together to promote right-wing agenda in America. Their major tools for this were a set of well-funded family foundations such as the Adolph Coors Foundation and the John M. Olin Foundation among others.

For the past two decades, these foundations have undertaken various activities to "sell" reactionary views: funding right-wing student newspapers, internships and endowed chairs for right-wing spokespersons on American campuses; supporting authors who write books hostile to American higher education; attempting to discredit social programs and other products of "liberal" thought; supporting conservative religious causes; lobbying for reactionary programs and ideologies in the Federal Congress and so forth.

Berliner and Biddle go on to say that the foundations above have also invested heavily in think tanks or institutes which they can count on to express their ideas. Berliner and Biddle identify the Heritage Foundation, the Hudson Institute, the American Enterprise Institute, the Hoover Institution, the Manhattan Institute and the Madder Center for Educational Affairs as some of the think tanks which, over the past twenty years, have had a remarkable impact on America.

Berliner and Biddle are careful to note that the reactionary movement is not monolithic, and they identify several ideological strands. The strands include: the classical conservativism of Edmund Burke; "economic rationalism"; "defense of the rich"; religious fundamentalism; suspicion of the Federal government; hostility to "public education and the academy (in general) and to social research (in particular)"; and racial, sexist, and ethnic bigotry. Berliner and Biddle identify three parts of this movement, to include the far right, the religious right, and the neo conservatives.

Berliner and Biddle identify the Heritage Foundation and such individuals as Edwin Meese, David Stockman, Warren Hatch and Jesse Helms as typical of the far right, who blame the federal government for most of the problems that are faced in American schools today, and who believe that all public expenditures are "inherently feckless or pernicious (pick one) and advocate reducing the entire public sector as a matter of policy." The far right has identified vested interests that they oppose to include "teacher's unions, educational associations, federal bureaucrats; racial, religious, and ethnic minorities; women and the disabled and homosexuals-indeed, presumably, anyone who is not WASP, male and straight."

Berliner and Biddle identify the religious right through organizations such as the Religious Roundtable, including individuals such as Jerry Falwell, Tim LeHay, Mel and Norma Gabler, and former presidential candidate Pat Robertson. According to Berliner and Biddle, "in general, the religious right argues that federal controls have been used to deny the students the 'right' to pray in schools; to restrict unfairly the teaching of 'scientific creationism'; to encourage the appearance of 'dirty,' 'anti-family', 'pro-homosexual' and 'anti-American' books and school curricula; and to enforce 'cultural relativity' in courses on values and sex education" (Berliner, p. 136). The end goal of the most extreme of the religious right is to eliminate public education altogether.

Finally, Berliner and Biddle identify the neo-conservatives through ties to such institutions as the American Enterprise Institute and through such publications as *Public Interest*, *Commentary*, and, more recently, *The New Republic*. Such individuals as William Bennett, Chester Finn, Lamar Alexander and Dianne Ravitch are among those who came to dominate federal education policy during the Reagan years and the Bush administration.

Berliner and Biddle identify common ideas among these three branches of the right. Despite their obvious differences, the three conservative ideologies we have reviewed share basic ideas about American education. All three are offended by recent changes in public schools and would like to return to mythic "golden years" when schools were more to their liking. All believe that public education has recently "deteriorated." All tend to be intolerant of the interests of minorities in education. All share a profound mistrust of both educators and students (the former are never portrayed as trustworthy professionals; the latter are never thought to be capable of self-motivated learning), and all blame "defects" in the public schools for problems in the larger society and propose changes in federal policy that will presumably cure those problems.

Not mentioned by Berliner and Biddle are related foundations, individuals and activities which include the recent publication of the anti-African *The Bell Curve* and its widespread dissemination throughout the media, including through some of the organs mentioned above. Significantly, *The Bell Curve* was written by co-author whose credentials include being a scholar with the American Enterprise Institute, a conservative think tank, with funding from another part of the network, the Bradley Foundation. Earlier, Alan Bloom had been sponsored by the Olin Foundation to write the vitriolic anti-African *Closing of the American Mind*. Linda Chavez of the American Enterprise Institute also edited an anti-African book, *Alternatives to Afrocentrism*, which was widely disseminated through mechanisms available to the wealthy and powerful. Finally, another writer associated with the American Enterprise Institute, Dinesh D'Souza, wrote a book so negative and, in my opinion, racist, oddly (or ironically) titled, *The End of Racism*, that two of the Black neo-conservatives, Robert Woodson and Glen Loury terminated their association with the American Enterprise Institute because of it.

Mary Lefkowitz's book, then, sponsored as it is by the Olin Foundation, which had also sponsored *The Closing of the American Mind*, is definitely a part of the genre of reactionary information peddling. It is also significant that, according to Martin Bernal, Mary Lefkowitz herself is advisor to the recently-formed National Association of Scholars, itself a right-wing group of "defenders of Western Civilization."

So let us be clear here. Any critique of *Not Out of Africa* must proceed from an awareness of this background. When Mary Lefkowitz challenges scholars with whom she disagrees with the phrase, "how Afrocentricity became an excuse to teach myth as history," then we must raise questions about her agenda and determine whether the story of the immaculate conception of Greco-Roman civilization is itself fact or myth.

The History of European Mythology About Africans in the Cloak of Scholarship

Any response to Mary Lefkowitz's book,   , must take into account the centuries of massive scholarly falsification of the history and culture of Africa and of people of

African descent throughout the world. This falsification is so massive, systematic, pervasive and continuing, that one can easily identify a wide body of literature documenting the details of the falsification process and the content. It is disingenuous of Lefkowitz, to say the least, to ignore the tragic record of this falsification and to fail to place the challenge of scholars whom she refers to as "Afro-centric" to falsification by European scholars in context. Is the African challenge a myth, or is it a challenge to myth'? A brief sampling of the actual record should suffice.

A summary statement about the fabrication, the falsification and the mythologizing about African history and culture were made by the outgoing president of the Organization of American Historians, Leon Litwack, Professor of History at the University of California, Berkeley. He cited past historians for perpetuating racism and asked that his present-day colleagues try to heal that wound: No group of scholars was more deeply implicated in the miseducation of American youth and did more to shape the thinking of generations of Americans about race and Blacks than historians. . . . Whether by neglect or distortion, the scholarly monographs and texts they authored perpetuated racial stereotypes and myths (Litwack, 1987).

What would make Litwack say such a thing? Any honest historian would find the answer very quickly, merely by reading the historical record itself. It requires little analysis. Jacob Carruthers (1995a) has looked at the cornerstone of Western ideology as reflected in "The Great Books of the Western World," first published in 1946. These books are portrayed as "the great conversation" and "the great ideas." For reasons articulated in the article by Carruthers, he refers to some of the Great Books of the Western World as "the curriculum of White supremacy" which was necessary for the creation of the condition that was asserted as the foundation of White supremacy, to provide a foundation for slavery and colonization. Since White supremacy did not exist, a curriculum was devised to bring it about; therefore the premise had to be taught, not only to Europeans but also to everybody else, especially Africans. In other words, the curriculum was designed to erase or ignore a significant portion of world history (Carruthers, 1995, pp. 31-32), especially Africa's part in it. Carruthers goes on to demonstrate the White supremacy content of some of the great books of the western world, one of which was written by Montesquieu, *Spirit of the Laws*. In Book 25, Volume 1 of Montesquieu's work, he says,

> "Were I to vindicate our right to make slaves of the Negroes, these would be my arguments: The Europeans, having extirpated the Americans, were obliged to make slaves of the Africans for clearing such vast tracks of land. Sugar would be too dear if the plants, which produce it, were cultivated by any other than slaves. These creatures are all-over Black, and with such a flat nose that they can scarcely be pitied. It is hardly to be believed that God, who is a wise being, should place a soul, especially a good soul, in such a Black, ugly body. The Negroes prefer a glass necklace to the gold which polite nations so highly value. Can there be a greater proof of their wanting common sense? It is natural to look upon color as the criterion of human nature. It is impossible for us to suppose these creatures to be men, because, allowing them to be men, a suspicion would follow that we ourselves are not Christian."
>
> (Carruthers, 1995 p. 32, citing Montesquieu)

According to Montesquieu, the human family could be divided into Savages, Barbarians and Civilized, with only the Europeans reaching the highest level. As a result, Montesquieu refers to Africa as follows: "The greatest part of the people of Africa . . . are savages and barbarians . . . they are without industry or arts . . . they have gold in abundance, which they receive immediately

57

from Nature. Every civilized state is therefore conditioned to traffic with them to advantage, by raising their esteem for things of no value, and receiving a very high price in return" (Carruthers, p. 33).

Another author of two of the great books of the western world was George Frederick Hegel. In his book, *The Philosophy of History*, Hegel describes Africa as such:

> "At this point we leave Africa not to mention it again, for it is not a historical part of the world; it has no movements or development to exhibit. Historical movements in it, that is in its northern part, belong to the Asiatic or European world. Carthage displayed there an important transitory phase of civilization; but, as a Phoenician colony, it belongs to Asia. Egypt will be considered in reference to its western phase, but it does not belong to the African spirit. What we properly understand by Africa is the unhistorical, undeveloped spirit, still involved in the conditions of mere nature, and which had to be presented here only as on the threshold of the world's history."
>
> (Carruthers, 1995, p. 34)

Only space requires that the actual citation of text be limited to these two authors. Thousands of other examples of European scholars, fabricating information about Africa and African people could be cited. Many authors have summarized this tradition of falsification. John Henrik Clarke has referred to it as Europe's "colonizing of world scholarship." Cheikh Anta Diop wrote an entire chapter on this falsification in his book, *The African Origin of Civilization*. The chapter was entitled, "The Modern Falsification of History." Martin Bernal, in his book *Black Athena*, wrote an entire chapter on the fabrication of the history of Ancient Greece. W. E. B. Du Bois in *Black Reconstruction* has a chapter on the propaganda of history. And finally, Arthur Schlesinger Senior and Junior are charged with falsification of the African experience (Jones, 1972). Arthur Schlesinger, Jr. is cited as justifying the use by government of "the royal lie" in order to achieve nationalistic aims, a concept, which by the way, goes all the way back to Plato.

And so, when Mary Lefkowitz and others pick a fight by challenging scholars whom she identifies as "Afrocentric" and charges them with making myth, we must situate in context such a challenge from the network that includes propagandizing for a political agenda, and also a network that includes a history of falsification. We do not need *characterization* of others from Mary Lefkowitz or any other Eurocentric scholar, what is needed, pure and simple, is d*ocumentation*. Only then will we be able to let the chips fall where they may.

We see a massive mobilization of money, press access, and pressure to promote anti African scholarship and to prevent African scholars from doing research on their own traditions. One thing is certain, however. The most dangerous threat to propaganda is not money, power or media access; it is merely a "whispering of the truth."

> Truth is all-potent with its silent power
> If only whispered, never heard aloud
> But working secretly, almost unseen
> Save in some excommunicated book;
> 'Tis as the lightning with its errand done
> Before you hear the thunder.
> —Gerald Massey (1974b, preface)

Mary Lefkowitz's basic problem: the Greek scholars as "Afrocentrists"

No matter how the texts are translated, the Greek texts themselves are full of the boasts of Greek scholars citing their debt to Egyptian teachers, to Kemetic teachers (Obenga, 1992; 1994; 1995). The general tradition of Western philosophy locates

Thales as the first Greek philosopher and scientist. This supposition precludes an inquiry as to the source of his intellectual perspectives. According to ancient historical testimonia, Thales received his education from priests in the Nile valley. These testimonia come from writers such as Diogenes, Laertius, Plato, Aetius, Proclus, Iamblichus and Plutarch, among others. This chapter, based on a very close scrutiny and exegesis of Greek texts, completely renews our understanding of Thales' association with Kemet (Obenga, 1995, p. 27).

One must understand that Egyptian antiquity was a period of wondrous progress. The ancient Greeks traced almost all human inventions to the Egyptians, from calculus, geometry, astronomy and dice games, to writing. The most ancient *(archaiotatoi)* of the human race *(ton anthropon)* would also be, by token of their anteriority with regard to civilization, the first creators of the human civilization recognized by Greece. Since the time of Homer, Egyptian antiquity functioned strictly as a highly memorialized component of Greek history. Herodotus said it, Plato confirmed it, and Aristotle never denied it.

The collective psychology of Greek scholars with regard to Egypt showed clearly that the Hellenic intellectual and cultural awakening cannot be taken out of its historical context: the Nile valley. The fame and anteriority of Egyptian civilization survives in part due to the writing of the Greek scholars of Mediterranean antiquity. There is nothing to do but state this fact and teach it as such (Obenga, 1995, p. 45). This classical record presents a serious problem; to deny it is to brand the Greek reporters as liars. Of course, this creates a credibility problem for the rest of the Greek record. There has been no satisfactory handling of this Greek record. The ancient record, in Greece and Kemet (Egypt), while lacking in many respects, leaves sufficient documentation for a prudent person to accept the Greek claim for their debt to Kemet.

In my opinion, this in no way diminishes the genius of the Greek people, anymore than it would the genius of any other people. Brilliant and wise people would seek the most developed tradition and the most developed science. It is through good fortune and hard work that people anywhere are able to advance beyond the narrow confines of present technologies and philosophies. It is time for Classicists in general to abandon embarrassment about the absence of an immaculate conception for Greek civilization. The fact that Asia may also have played a part in no way minimizes the simple fact that we must look to cultural antecedents in order to explain Greece. The fact that Greece is not an exact mirror of its antecedents is in no way a challenge to the existence of those antecedents. One would expect modifications consistent with new environment.

Does Mary Lefkowitz avoid the most relevant scholarship?

Mary Lefkowitz arbitrarily segregates in what I believe to be a most racist way the scholarship that exists. She separates it into "Afrocentric" and presumably non-Afrocentric scholarship, supposedly meaning Black scholarship and White scholarship. The problem is that many of the people that Mary Lefkowitz refers to as "Afrocentrists" have never referred to themselves in the same way. In fact, some explicitly reject the designation, among scholars of African descent. Moreover, many of the people who make the arguments that Mary Lefkowitz identifies as Afrocentric are European scholars, such as Sir Basil Davidson, Count Volney and Gerald Massey, not to mention Martin Bernal. The Lefkowitz use of labeling and characterization of scholarship, with its feeble criteria, has more of the ring of propaganda than scholarship.

But most significant is her ignorance of, or avoidance of, some of the best scholarship on this question. Clearly the work of Theophile Obenga, the student and colleague of the great Cheikh Anta Diop, who is fluent in Kemetic as well as Greek, and who

61

has written extensively on these matters, should be familiar to Lefkowitz. His detailed scholarly work, however, is not mentioned in her book at all (Obenga, 1989; 1992; 1994; 1995). Mary Lefkowitz chooses instead to cite the older text of George G. M. James (which is still an excellent reference by one whose citations are virtually all European historians of philosophy), or unnamed students in classes that she has observed. As I read *Not Out of Africa*, Lefkowitz misses the main body of relevant scholarship or chooses not to deal with that part of it, which she seems to know about, specifically the work of Cheikh Anta Diop. Diop's work cannot easily be characterized. It must be read and discussed point by point, something that Lefkowitz does not do.

The grand circumstances.

Certain things are clear and unmistakable. One of which is the time line, the actual chronology of events. Kemet was older and more highly developed than Greece by thousands of years. One need only note that by the time the Greek philosophers appear in Greek history, generously around the sixth century B.C.E., Kemet was already old and grey, having itself already developed philosophy, the scientific method, mathematics, and astronomy (Obenga, 1989; 1992; 1994; 1995).

With the time line, we also note Greek contact with Kemet, by both the Greek and Kemetic record. And finally, the record is clear on the Greek use of Kemet. The Kemetic religion was a major influence in Greece (Boyd, 1991; Brady, 1935; Heyob, 1975; Hicks, 1962; Massey, 1974b; Obenga, 1995; Politt, 1965; Scott, 1987; Solmsen, 1979; Witt, 1971). The architecture of Greece must be compared to that of millennia-old architecture in Kemet. The scientific approach of Kemet must be compared to that of Greece. Any honest use of the time line, the contact and the record of Greek development post Kemetic contact do not support Lefkowitz at all!

"The Myth of the Immaculate Conception of Western Civilization"
Asa G. Hilliard, III
Georgia State University

Conclusion

Mary Lefkowitz either is ignorant of, ignores or understates the arguments that oppose her position. One simple illustration is to characterize the great Dr. Cheikh Anta Diop as "Senegal's humanist and scientist." Dr. Lefkowitz fails to mention that Dr. Diop was uniquely qualified to deal precisely with the matters that she seeks to challenge. Dr. Diop earned his Ph.D. in Egyptology from the University of Paris, Sorbonne. In the course of his higher education, he had formal study and practical experience with the great physicists and chemists of Europe, himself directing the radiocarbon dating laboratory in Dakar Senegal. Moreover, Dr. Diop was highly trained in anthropology, including physical anthropology, and was even a linguist of note. Further, he was a historian and had an unusually developed grasp of political economy. He was uniquely qualified to integrate a variety of relevant Academic disciplines. His intimate knowledge of continental African culture as well as his intimate knowledge of European continental culture, including the ancient past of both, makes him an unparalleled expert in the study of Kemet and Greece.

It is unfortunate, but it is a fact of life, that the documentation which challenges the unfounded media blitzkrieg on African scholars in particular, and European scholars who agree with them in general, has little access to the mass media that carries the unrebutted assault of the academic muggers. Big money buys slick publications and media access. But truth whispered is, "like lightning with its errand done," before we hear the thunder.

Selected References

Berliner, D. C.; & Biddle, B. J. (1995). *The Manufactured Crisis: Myth. Fraud and the attack on America's Public Schools*. New York: Addison-Wesley Publishers.

Boyd, P. C. (1991). *The African Origin of Christianity: A Biblical and Historical Account*. London: Karia Press.

Brady, T. A. (1935). The Reception of the Egyptian Cult by the Greeks, 330-30 B.C. *The University of Missouri Studies: A Quarterly of Research*, (1). Columbia: The University of Missouri.

Browder, A. (1992). *Nile Valley Contributors to Civilization: Exploding the Myths*, Vol. I. Washington D.C.: Institute for Karmic Guidance.

Carruthers, J. H. (1995a). *MDW NTR Divine Speech: A Historiographical Reflection of African Thought from the Time of the Pharaohs to the Present*. London: Karnak House.

Carruthers, J. H. (1995b). Reflections on the History of African Education. *Illinois Schools Journal*, 7(1), 25-39.

Diop, C. A. (1991). *Civilization or Barbarism: An Authentic Anthropology*. Brooklyn, N.Y.: Lawrence Hill Books.

Dow, S. (1937). The Egyptian Cults of Athens. *Harvard Theological Review*, 183-232.

Harris, J.R. (Ed.). (1971). *The Legacy of Egypt*. Oxford: Clarendon Press.

Heyob, S. K. (1975). *The Cult of Isis among Women in the Greco-Roman World.* Leiden: E.J. Brill.

Hicks, R. I. (1962). Egyptian Elements in Greek Mythology. *Transactions of the American Philosophical Association,* 106-107.

Jackson, J. G. (1971). *Christianity before Christ.* Austin Texas: American Atheist Press. 17.

Jones, S. (1972). The Schlesingers on Black History. *Phylon,* ~(2), 104-111.

Litwack, L. (1987). *Black Issues in Higher Education.*

Magie, D. (1955). Egyptian Deities in Asia Minor in inscriptions and on coins. *American Journal of Archaeology,* (3), 163-187.

Massey, G. (1974a). *A Book of the Beginnings (2 Vols.).* New Jersey: University Books Inc.

Massey, G. (1974b). *Ancient Egypt: The Light of the World (2 Vols.)* New York: Samuel Weiser.

Obenga, T. (1989). African Philosophy of the Pharaonic Period. In I. Van Sertima (Ed.). *Egypt Revisited.* (pp. 277-285). New Brunswick: Transaction.

Obenga, T. (1992). *Ancient Egypt and Black Africa: A student's handbook for the study of Ancient Egypt in philosophy, linguistics and gender relations.* Chicago: U.S. Office and Distributors: Front Line International (Chicago, Illinois).

Obenga, T. (1994). *Major Issues in Ancient Egyptian scholarship.* Unpublished manuscript.

Obenga, T. (1995). *A Lost Tradition: African Philosophy in World History*. Philadelphia: The Source Editions.

Parker, G. W. (1917). The African origin of the Grecian civilization. *Journal of Negro History*, 2, 334-344.

Politt, J. J. (1965). The Egyptian Gods in Attica: Some epigraphical evidence. *J-Iesperia*; L4, 125-130.

Sauneron, S. (1969). *The Priests of Ancient Egypt*. New York.

Scott, T. M. (1987). *Egyptian Elements in Hermetic Literature: A thesis*. Cambridge: Harvard Divinity School. Dissertation.

Smith, E. M. (1928). The Egypt of the Greek Romances. *The Classical Journal*, _2~(7) 531-537.

Solmsen, F. (1979). *Isis Among the Greeks and Romans*. Cambridge: Harvard University Press.

Witt, R. E. (1971). *Isis in the Greco-Roman World*. New York: Cornell University Press.

In and Out of Africa: Misreading Afrocentricity
Charles Verharen
Howard University

Philosophy's most powerful methodology is to show someone wrong on her own grounds. In the subtitle of *Not Out of
Africa*, Mary Lefkowitz has claimed that Afrocentricity is "an
excuse to teach myth as history." However in the very process of
constructing arguments for her position she undermines it. Her
arguments commit her to several hypotheses that are remarkable
for their Afrocentric character: the Greeks themselves were the
world's earliest Afrocentrists (Lefkowitz, 1996, pp. 53-58), ancient Egyptians can accurately be called people of color
(Lefkowitz, 1996, 13); the Egyptians influenced Greek culture
over a long period of time in unspecified ways (Lefkowitz, 1996,
p. 161); and Egyptian and other African cultures exhibit remarkable similarities (Lefkowitz, 1992, 135).

With these three theses, Lefkowitz displays a nascent Afrocentric philosophy. She also begins to commit herself to an Afrocentric research methodology. She admits that whenever she
teaches classics in the future, she will not fail to mention the Afrocentric hypothesis: "In my own case I would never teach Plato
again without mentioning the Afrocentrist theory that Socrates
was of African descent, and in all my courses I discuss the question of Egyptian influence on Greece" (Lefkowitz, 1996, p. 64).
Of course the mere mention of these issues is not sufficient to be
called truly Afrocentric. Nevertheless, Lefkowitz has committed
herself to certain ideas that might over time yield results.

In her overt remarks, Lefkowitz espouses a Eurocentric methodology whose principles have been fixed over the past several
centuries. She looks at African experience through European eyes,
and cannot see a major African influence on Greek culture. But her
parenthetical remarks open up a new way to read her text. This
essay's first part will reflect on two varieties of Afrocentricity.

 67

The second part will examine Lefkowitz' reasons for dismissing Diop's Afrocentric claims. The third part will consider arguments for Egyptian ontology's sophistication. The fourth part will address Afrocentricity's research method.

The essay's conclusion will discuss the consequences of Lefkowitz' position for African American life. Lefkowitz worries about Afrocentricity's consequences for Greek sensibilities (Lefkowitz, 1996, p. 168). But she must consider how her own work follows the European tradition of denying African contributions to world culture. With Hegel, Lefkowitz rallies around the call: Not out of Africa. Her research philosophy undermines African American self-images, and thwarts research that would look for lines of cultural continuity stretching from an African past to the global present.

Lefkowitz' Eurocentric Afrocentricity

The deconstruction of Lefkowitz' version of Afrocentricity must start with her definition. She argues that in his *Stolen Legacy* G.M. James, a founding father of Afrocentricity in her eyes, constructs an Egypt that is Greco-Roman rather than African (Lefkowitz, 1996, pp. 135, 136). Her primary claim is that Afrocentricity is Eurocentric in its most basic form: "Another Eurocentric feature of Afrocentricity is its concentration on Egypt. By failing to pay equal regard to other African civilizations, such as that of Nubia, the Afrocentrists appear to be judging African cultures by European standards. Egypt has always been admired by Europeans for the antiquity of its civilization and for its artistic and architectural remains. Why focus on one African nation that has won European admiration for its achievements? Extreme Afrocentricity prevents students from learning about real ancient African civilizations" (Lefkowitz, 1996, p. 156).

Of course Lefkowitz is no reader of Cheikh Anta Diop and earlier scholars who have demonstrated that a study of all African civilizations is a must for scholarship. Indeed, there is no dearth of studies on African civilizations. What is at the root of Lefkowitz' concern is the issue of Egypt itself and nothing more. She claims mistakenly that for Afrocentrists to focus on Egypt is somehow to look at civilization from the standpoint of Europe. This is one more example of the assumption that any study of Egypt must be governed by Eurocentric criteria. Her own research methodology dictates that since Egypt is in Africa, we must look to Africa herself for a true definition of Egypt: "To learn about Africa we must look where the Afrocentrists fail to look, that is, to the historical Egypt described by the ancient Egyptians themselves, and to the important cultural links to neighboring parts of Africa" (Lefkowitz, 1996, p. 135).

If Lefkowitz paid careful attention to Cheikh Anta Diop, the Afrocentrist who devoted his career to careful examination of the "historical Egypt," she would have found that he had anticipated her advice: "For us, the return to Egypt in all domains is the necessary condition for reconciling African civilizations with history, in order to be able to construct a body of modern human sciences, in order to renovate African culture. Far from being a reveling in the past, a look toward the Egypt of antiquity is the best way to conceive and build our cultural future. In reconceived and renewed African culture, Egypt will play the same role that Greco-Roman antiquity plays in Western culture" (Lefkowitz, 1996, pp. 135, 136). Lefkowitz foregoes mentioning that information about African and Egyptian cultural commonalties was very likely not available to James since the anthropological search for them has begun only recently.

As Lefkowitz' criticism of James makes clear, some Afrocentric scholarship departs from forms of Eurocentric professionalism as it has been defined by some scholars. What escapes Lefkowitz is the character of the scholarship that has led to the contemporary definition of Afrocentricity. As St. Clair Drake's *Black Folk Here and There* indicates, Afrocentricity is an idea (if not a name) that dates back to the early 1800's. The extent of lay research into the history and agency of Africans is vast indeed. George James' work was achieved while he was a professor at the University of Arkansas-Pine Bluff, but his warrant for the research was based entirely in the historical and research achievements of African communities. Lefkowitz confuses Afrocentricity with a discussion of research on African sources and civilization. The idea that George James had a notion of the definition of Afrocentricity or would have called himself one is highly speculative. Everyone who writes on the significance of ancient Egypt for African cultures is not necessarily an Afrocentrist.

Diop's Afrocentricity

As Diop indicates in the introduction to *Civilization or Barbarism*, his final and most powerful work, his theory of the African origin of civilization is grounded in the idea that all cultures have a continuity that can be traced back to an original African origin. The African origin of civilization is important because it relates to the development of human approaches to culture and the survival of the human species. Thus, Diop's concern with the African origin of civilization might be seen as related to the more modern idea of Afrocentricity, which includes but is not limited to discourse around the origin of civilization. In the past, cultures have distanced themselves from one another by tactics of de-humanization, even demonization. Diop claims that given the destructive powers of contemporary civilization, we can only survive by renouncing the barbarism of cultural divisiveness for the sake of a new global concept of civilization: "Today each group of people, armed with its rediscovered or reinforced cultural identity, has arrived at the threshold of the post-industrial era. An atavistic, but vigilant, African optimism inclines us to wish that all nations would join hands in order to build a planetary civilization instead of sinking down to barbarism" (Diop, 1992, p. 7).

Diop believes that all nations must contribute to this planetary civilization, and the common ground for all their efforts must be scientific methodology. So attached to a common methodology is Diop that his preliminary conviction about the primacy of African cultures derives from European scholarship. In principle, Lefkowitz can refute Diop by showing that the tools of contemporary classical scholarship refute the Afrocentric hypotheses. Lefkowitz' reviewer, Glen Bowersock, summarizes this position:

> "The standard scholarly position on Egypt and the Greeks goes as follows: The Greeks had great respect for Egyptian culture, which was older than theirs, and they observed parallels in their religion and thought to what they found in Egypt. So they supposed that they had borrowed from the Egyptians. However, in the 20th century we can show with the analytical tools of scholarship (above all, source criticism and documentary material such as inscriptions, coins and papyri) that they were wrong. I subscribe to this position, but we have to admit that it cannot be promulgated as proven fact."
>
> (Bowersock, 1992, p. 7)

Bowersock's language is instructive. The Greeks suffered under an Afrocentric illusion that "they had borrowed from the Egyptians." But contemporary scholarly tools have produced no evidence of specific cultural transfer. But, as Bowersock admits, absence of evidence is not evidence of absence. The "not out of Africa" hypothesis "cannot be promulgated as proven fact."

Lefkowitz points out mistakes in the Afrocentric hypothesis of the ancient Greeks, but nowhere does she admit in Bowersock's refreshing phrase that her thesis "cannot be promulgated as proven fact." What Lefkowitz fails to consider carefully is Diop's evidence for the Afrocentric thesis. Taking his lead from the French scholar Emile Amelineau, Diop argues that the Timaeus, one of the most important texts in Greek philosophy, cannot be understood without using the Egyptian philosophical concepts on which it is based. Lefkowitz addresses Diop's claims about this text but she

 71

dismisses any possibility of deep structural dependence. Her fundamental research hypothesis is that superficial similarities in texts must be based on coincidence rather than cultural lineage. Lefkowitz argues that the similarities between Greek and Egyptian cosmologies are not products of cultural diffusion, but accidents of spontaneous, independent origination. Criticizing Diop's idea that Heraclitus received his theory of opposites from Egyptian priests, for example, she claims that "the notion of opposites can be found in virtually any religious text, because it is a fundamental mode of human thought" (Lefkowitz, 1996, pp. 152-153).

The philosophical issue here is the set of assumptions driving research in the two cultures. Lefkowitz's paradigm precludes a search for patterns of cultural diffusion because of her assumption of independent origination for analogous cultural features. She would support her primary hypothesis with cross-cultural comparisons that show the multiplicity of cultural analogues. Diop's paradigm is one of cultural diffusion. He would point to the same evidence in support of his hypothesis. Diop's paradigm drives him to look for identity, while Lefkowitz searches for difference. These paradigms reflect radically different temperaments. Fortunately, the difference abets rather than thwarts good scholarship.

Lefkowitz marshalls her argument against Diop's specific claim in the Timaeus in the following way: "With much ingenuity, Diop attempts to show that Plato's Timaeus is heavily dependent on Egyptian ideas, which Plato learned during his thirteen-year visit to Heliopolis. The "proof" that Plato is transmitting Egyptian ideas is that in the Timaeus Plato says the world was created by a demiurge, and that Ra, the god of Heliopolis, was also said to have created the world. Like James, Diop assumes that the existence of common themes is a proof of dependency" (Lefkowitz, 1996, pp. 151, 152).

Diop claims much more than a vague similarity between Ra and Plato's demiurge. He cites four points of comparison. First, neither Ra nor Plato's demiurge "create" the world in the sense of bringing it into a state of existence from a state of non-existence. Second, in both cosmogonies the "world" as formless matter in a chaotic state served as a primordial matter to be restructured by an "ordering" rather than a "creating" god. Third, the "blueprint" for bringing unformed matter into the structured universe exists in an independent way for both Plato and the Egyptians. The divine essences, the "forms" of Plato are the templates that the demiurge consults in ordering the universe, just as Ma'at is the divine order of a universe brought to perfection by Ra's ministrations. Fourth, the fundamental ontologies of Plato and the Egyptians are identical: a primordial matter, a set of ordering principles, and a divine intelligence that brings chaotic matter to perfect form (Diop, 1992, p. 337-353).

If Diop could only cite one resemblance between the Greek and Egyptian cosmogonies, then Lefkowitz' criticism would be quite telling. It is plausible that a single idea might evolve independently in two separate cultures. For example, her criticism of Diop's claim that Heraclitus "law of opposites" must be Egyptian in origin is plausible. In her words, Diop fails to "observe that the notion of opposites can be found in virtually any religious text, because it is a fundamental mode of human thought" (Diop, 1992, p. 153).

However, Diop's work on the Timaeus cites four points of striking similarity, though Lefkowitz mentions only one of them. Diop also makes broad claims for other points of resemblance: "archetypes..., the worldsoul, immortality of the world-soul and of the individual soul..., theory of the four elements—earth, fire, air, water, mathematical essence of the world conceived as a pure number, metempsychosis, the soul of the stars, sphere of the fixed stars, celestial equator, ecliptic, theory of the movement of the planets" (Diop, 1992, p. 340). Diop does not pursue these possible points of resemblance in any detail because his method is philosophical rather than detail-oriented. But he assumes that other scholars have explored this ground thoroughly enough to lend weight to his claims. In particular Diop cites the classicist Emile Amelineau who argued that Plato did not simply copy Egyptian texts but "interpreted" them "with incomparable brilliance" (Diop, 1992, p. 341).

Amelineau's work has had no lasting effect on current scholarship in the classics, but that is not evidence that his hypothesis of Egyptian influence on Greek thought is wrong. Lefkowitz' summary dismissal of the hypothesis is not grounded in scholarship but rather in her own philosophical conviction. In her view, any resemblance between Greek and Egyptian cosmogonies must be coincidental: "Even if the Greek philosophers actually went to Egypt, they did not steal their philosophy during their visits there. The important Egyptian religious texts share only a few general common themes with the Greek philosophical writings, most of which can be found in the religious works of other ancient Mediterranean peoples" (Lefkowitz, 1996, p. 157). But can it be only coincidence that both cosmogonies share four primary features (no creation ex nihilo, raw material, structure, and architect)? Perhaps, but without investigation a hypothesis of cultural diffusion seems quite as robust as one of independent origination.

Egyptian Ontological Sophistication

Lefkowitz also discusses another point of comparison between the ontologies of the Egyptians and Aristotle. Arguing against James' claim that Aristotle's concept of the unmoved mover was "stolen" from Memphite theology, Lefkowitz claims that Aristotle's "abstract theology" can have nothing in common with "the anthropomorphic creator god Ptah of the Memphite Theology. All that the two texts have in common is a concern with creation of the universe" (Lefkowitz, 1996, p. 141).

Here Lefkowitz may be guilty of venturing out of her own field of expertise. Erik Hornung in Conceptions of God in Ancient Egypt remarks on the folly of underestimating Egyptian philosophical sophistication. Thinkers throughout the ages have belittled Egyptian anthropomorphic representations of the gods without exploring their allegorical possibilities.

"In and Out of Africa: Misreading Afrocentricity"
Charles Verharen
Howard University

Hornung cites an ancient dialogue between Momus and Zeus to remind us of the perils of underestimating Egyptian sophistication: Momus: "But you, you dog-faced Egyptian, dressed-up in linen, who do you think you are, my friend? How do you expect to pass for a god, when you howl as you do?" Zeus: "These things you observe about the Egyptians are truly shocking. All the same, Momus, the greater part of them has a mystic significance, and it's not all right to laugh at them, just because you are not one of the initiated" (Lucian, 2nd cent AD, Deorum concilium quoted in Hornung, 1982, p. 15).

Hornung claims that Egyptian ontology is so sophisticated that we require concepts from contemporary physics and logic to comprehend its logical structure (Hornung, 1982, pp. 273-274). For Hornung, Egyptian cosmology explains not only the origin of the gods and the universe, but also the emergence of being from non-being. If Hornung is correct about Egyptian sophistication, Lefkowitz oversteps the bounds of her research field. She admits that this mistake is a common temptation: "As a classicist, I may overemphasize the achievement of the Greeks because 1 do not know enough about the rest of the Mediterranean world; Egyptologists may be inclined to make the same mistake in the opposite direction. We recognize that no historian can write without some amount of bias; that is why history must always be rewritten" (Lefkowitz, 1996, p.161). But Lefkowitz's principles for rewriting history deserve careful scrutiny.

Afrocentric Methodology

In her concluding remarks Lefkowitz asks whether Afrocentricity is a new historical methodology (Lefkowitz, 1996, p.158). She believes that Afrocentricity's primary problem derives from its reliance on cultural relativism. Her definition of cultural relativism makes it an epistemology whereby cultural interests assume far more weight in research than does historical evidence. She claims that Afrocentrists like Asante and Diop construct histories that pay no attention to available evidence; "Asante

75

appears to be saying that no one need believe anything that any European says about Africa" (Lefkowitz, 1996, pp. 7, 59).

Neither Diop nor Asante subscribe to such a research methodology. As I indicated above, much of Diop's interpretation of Egyptian texts is based on European scholarship. For Diop there can be only one research methodology, namely that of science. Science is a system of generalizations that must be tested through experience. No claim can stand without evidence, and the evidence must be consensual across cultures. Diop's keen interest in the implications of quantum mechanics (especially multi-valued logics and the Bell Theorem) shows the extent of his philosophical reflection on the scientific method (Diop, 1992, pp. 368-375).

Diop's treatment of historical evidence is couched in the philosophy of science of his day. This literature called the very nature of a fact into question by claiming that all facts are theory laden. Evidence cannot stand-alone but must be interpreted in the context of a theory. Theories in their turn do not rise and fall on the basis of evidence alone. Evidence must be interpreted in light of the background assumptions supporting the theory. The dispute between geo-centrists and helio-centrists furnishes a classical example of the complex relations between theory, evidence, and background assumptions. The apparent evidence for both theories was the same: the sun appears to wheel through the sky. The more subtle evidence was also the same: the best scientific instruments of the times had failed to detect stellar parallax (the apparent motion of the fixed stars due to the real motion of the earth).

The parties to the dispute differed primarily in their background assumptions. The heliocentrists had to assume that parallax could not be detected because the nearest stars were astronomical distances from the observer's position. The instruments of the time were too coarse to detect parallax over such extreme distances. The geo-centrists did not imagine that such distances were plausible. Basing their ideas in the moral and spiritual grounding of the culture, the geo-centrists believed that anything that contradicted their belief in the centrality of the earth could not be possible.

Interpretation of the Evidence

Both parties paid equal attention to the evidence, but it was the assumptions grounded in imagination and buoyed up by conviction that dictated the proper interpretation of the evidence. Neither side had any means for measuring the distance from the solar system to the fixed stars, so neither party had any evidence for its presuppositions. The final resolution of the dispute depended on instruments capable of detecting stellar parallax. These did not become available until F. Bessel's work in 1838.

Theories, whether historical or scientific, are systems for representing experience. In Wittgenstein's felicitous metaphor, theories are like maps. They can represent their terrain or their "evidence" by quite different means of projection. Like hypotheses, maps do not yield "truth" but are simply better or worse suited for their purposes. No map, however, can completely disregard the terrain, just as no hypothesis can disregard the evidence. Lefkowitz' claim that Afrocentrists dispense with evidence for the sake of a higher cultural "truth" pays no attention to Diop's lifelong efforts to find evidence corroborating his hypothesis about the African origins of civilization. Her cries of "cultural relativism" should not obscure the true nature of her conflict with Diop. The argument is not so much about evidence, as about the philosophical motive to look for evidence. European classical scholars and Afrocentrists cite the same evidence for their hypotheses about Greek dependence on Egyptian thought. Nineteenth century classicists separated Egypt from Greece for reasons of good scholarship—no documents or other supporting material grounded the ancient Greek conviction that their culture owed much to Egypt.

Afrocentrists, on the other hand, argue that Greek texts citing Greek dependence on Egypt are accurate. Both parties cite the same texts in support of their hypotheses. Have recent tools of scholarship developed new evidence? No scholars conversant in both Egyptology and classics have conducted careful research that would link Hornung's claims for extraordinary sophistication in Egyptian cosmology to Diop's arguments about our inability to understand the *Timaeus* without a background knowledge of Egyptian cosmology.

Lefkowitz would be impatient with calls for further research on the question because of her philosophical conviction that no evidence will ever be found to support Afrocentricity. She considers the question closed. She cannot admit that Afrocentrists might have a legitimate philosophical difference with her point of view. For her, the only reason for Afrocentricity's rise in the academies is a pernicious cultural relativism.

Like Dinesh d'Souza in the *End of Racism*, Lefkowitz blames the powerful influence of a new breed of cultural relativist scholars for what is wrong with academia: "Instructors in universities now place less emphasis on the acquisition of factual information than they did a generation ago. They are suspicious of the value of facts, or to put it another way, they think that facts are meaningless because they can be manipulated and reinterpreted" (Lefkowitz, 1996, p. 48). For Lefkowitz, cultural relativism implies that there can be many diverse "truths" (Lefkowitz, 1996, p. 162).

Lefkowitz agrees with the contemporary commonplace that all facts are theory laden. Nearly every history includes "bias of some sort" and no historical account can be "entirely accurate." However, historians have always known that they write "with an evident bias" (Lefkowitz, 1996, p.48). However, Lefkowitz thinks that cultural relativism puts a new spin on this old healthy skepticism about historical facts. If societal values engender "unconscious" bias, then history must be regarded as a "cultural projection" of social values "whether individual writers are aware of it or not" (Lefkowitz, 1996, p. 49). Cultural relativism "make[s] it possible to say that all history is by definition fiction" (Lefkowitz, 1996, p. 49).

What Lefkowitz misses is that while values may well be cultural artifacts, they also serve as springs of action. Values dictate both aims and methods. In science, experience dictates the limit to reading nature in terms of any given cultural perspective. But there can be no difference in science and history with respect to the importance of evidence. Historians submit their claims to the test of consensual experience in the same manner as scientists. This is not to say that consensus yields "truth."

Diop would never argue, as Lefkowitz claims he must as an Afrocentrist, that "history is fiction" or that evidence is not important to history. But Lefkowitz claims that Diop is constructing historical fiction according to his own taste. History is reduced to mere aesthetics: "The inevitable result of cultural history-writing, unless it is done with the greatest of caution, is a portrait of the past painted with broad strokes and bright colors of our own choosing" (Lefkowitz, 1996, p. 49).

With this language Lefkowitz dismisses the freedom of choice that characterizes all forms of representation. We must choose our methods of representation, our "strokes and colors." Whether the strokes are too broad or the colors too bright is a matter for philosophical decision, not historical or scientific precision. A research program must be based on a system that picks out and assigns weight to evidence. The system does not consist in a random association of facts. It is a whole campaign for discovering and arranging facts. The best case a research program is a campaign that we choose with deliberation rather than unconscious cultural motives. Research programs spring from "bright colors of our own choosing" because we must have a vivid picture of the enterprise and its possible results if we are to have the motivation necessary to carry out a lengthy and arduous process.

Diop's research program on the hypothesis of African origins consumed his whole life.

Lefkowitz has difficulty conceiving the enormity of the work called for by the Afrocentric research program. She expects the evidence for Afrocentricity to be almost intuitively obvious to a casual researcher. She claims, for example, that it should be easy to find concrete evidence of an Egyptian influence on Greek culture in the very nature of Egyptian thought: "If the Greeks had learned their philosophy from a large body of theoretical literature produced by Egyptian writers, surely some trace of that literature would have remained in Egypt, and we would know the names or schools that produced it. We have a detailed knowledge of Greek literature, even though the Romans used it as the model for their own original literary creations" (Lefkowitz, 1996, p. 158). Lefkowitz ignores the fact that scholars have had access to Greek and Roman literature since the time of its origination. European scholarship on Egyptian texts dates back only to the first part of the 19th century. Lefkowitz also passes over the fact that research takes money and time. Determination, "bright colors," "broad strokes" are not enough to mount a full-scale research program.

Ignoring the enormous logistical problems Afrocentric research has faced, Lefkowitz cavalierly dismisses Afrocentrists as cultural relativists whose social commitments have blinded them to historical evidence. She pleads for their return to the objectivist fold: "...once we accept the idea that instead of truth, there are many truths, or different ethnic truths, we cannot hope to have an intellectual community. This is why we cannot each remain in our own separate enclaves without talking with colleagues who share similar interests and concerns" (Lefkowitz, 1996, pp. 174, 175). But if scholars had a perfect community of "similar interests and concerns," scholarship could never advance past the limits of inherent bias.

The extraordinary bias of European scholars against Africa should serve as an example to prevent scholars from looking for too much "community of interest." Lefkowitz admits that cultural or ethnic concerns may animate certain kinds of research: "...a person of African descent may be more curious about the civilization of ancient Egypt than someone from another ethnic background. But African ancestry alone will not help him understand ancient Egyptian religion or enable him to read hieroglyphics. As we have seen, it did not prevent Diop from imagining that Mystical Egypt was a reality" (Lefkowitz, 1996, p. 167).

But Lefkowitz has only to remind herself of the effects of European bias on African scholarship. Lefkowitz rejects Asante's claim that Europe's vision of Africa could not be objective: "the objectivity of knowledge referred to by European scholars could not be separated from the consciousness of the social-cultural world and...Europeans brought that consciousness with them whenever they discussed Africa" (Lefkowitz, 1996, p.159).

Lefkowitz glosses Asante's quote aggressively: "Asante appears to be saying that no one need believe anything that any Europeans says about Africa. That declaration is indeed liberating, at least to Afrocentrists. Anyone who accepts Asante's formulation need not trust a word I have said in this book, or that anyone has said or will ever say in criticism of Afrocentricity" (Lefkowitz, 1996, p.159). A more sympathetic reader of Asante would interpret his remark in the context of a specific piece of European scholarship on Africa. Hegel's work on Africa is perhaps the single best example. Did Hegel 'bring his European consciousness with him whenever he discussed Africa'? In his primary research on Africa, Hegel claimed that Greece was far more sophisticated than Egypt, but also that Greece was dependent on Egyptian culture. Hegel also foreclosed on any possibility of deep cultural connections between Egypt and Nubia, and these two areas with the rest of Africa. Hegel's research hypothesis was purely philosophical rather than historical. It was based not on examination of historical evidence but rather on the Egyptomania consequent upon Napoleon's invasion of Egypt and Champollion's deciphering of the Rosetta stone. But what are the consequences of Hegel's philosophical position, immersed as it was in racist European consciousness? Hegel proclaimed this philosophical stance in the 1800's and he was merely following up on the prior claims of Hume and Kant that "real" Africans were not capable of fully human abstraction. Hegel's research program would prevent any serious research into Egyptian sophistication or connections with the rest of Africa.

But Lefkowitz herself now claims that Egypt has cultural ties to other parts of Africa and that research should be conducted in this area. How has her own "European consciousness" changed? Lefkowitz makes a plea for a globally enlarged consciousness that would suppress research driven by purely cultural reasons: "Rather than assume that each race, or each ethnic group, or each nation, should write its own versions of history, I would ... [call] for a wider cosmopolitanism, which seeks to be sensitive to different points of view, and which can represent a diversity of viewpoints" (Lefkowitz, 1996, p.160). But she simply cannot accept the possibility that the fundamental Afrocentric hypothesis of African origins should be included in her "wider cosmopoli-tanism."

Lefkowitz states that cosmopolitanism can only be stretched so far: "There are of course many possible interpretations of the truth, but some things are simply not true" (Lefkowitz, 1996, p. 161). She cites the idea that there was no Holocaust as an example of something that simply cannot be true. But she also claims that the Afrocentric idea is another example of something that cannot possibly be true. The difference in the kinds of research programs that would generate statements about the Holocaust and Afrocentricity are extraordinary, but she cites them as comparable examples; "Likewise, it is not true that the Greeks stole their philosophy from Egypt; rather, it is true that the Greeks were influenced in various ways over a long period of time by their contact with the Egyptians" (Lefkowitz, 1996, p. 161).

Here Lefkowitz acknowledges the truth of Afrocentricity's primary claim about Greece. But she dodges the need for careful scholarship on the exact extent of this influence by claiming that Egyptian culture was not sophisticated enough to influence Greek culture in major ways. She disguises the controversial nature of her claim by displacing attention onto James' radical hypothesis: "But then, what culture at any time has not been influenced by other cultures, and what exactly do we mean by "influence"? If we talk about Greek philosophy as a "Stolen Legacy," which the Greeks swiped from Egyptian universities, we are not telling the truth, but relating a story, or a myth, or a tall tale. But if we talk about Egyptian influence on Greece, we are discussing a historical issue" (Lefkowitz, 1996, p. 161).

Lefkowitz is aware that academic research programs may have social consequences, but she passes lightly over their dangers: "Of course, teaching false information about Socrates and Aristotle will not put anyone in immediate physical danger. But nonetheless these untruths do injustice, not only to the ancient Greeks who have been falsely maligned, but also to their descendants. Why deprive the Greeks of their heritage, particularly if the charges against the ancient Greeks can decisively be shown to be wrong? Why encourage hostility toward any ethnic group? Haven't we see enough examples in the century of the horrific results of teaching hostile propaganda" (Lefkowitz, 1996, p. 168)?

How can Lefkowitz pass over historical examples where teaching false information has put people in the gravest physical danger? Perhaps she might review the consequences of Hegel's research program for African peoples. Hegel's and other Europeans' "false information" about Africans was part and parcel of European efforts to put Africans "in immediate physical danger." It was not simply a question of `depriving Africans of their heritage. It was a deliberate attempt to use a false image of Africans to destroy African possibilities. That false image is still

83

very powerful in contemporary consciousness, and it is in no way based on a careful examination of African life.

Afrocentricity is a deliberate attempt on the part of Africans on the continent and in the Diaspora to scrutinize that false image in detail. Under Hegel's research program, Europeans simply had no reason to examine the African evidence, since it was evident that Africans were not human. If Europeans used a false image of Africa to enslave Africans, what could motivate them to pay careful attention to African culture? The motives for Hegel's anti-African animus are easy to imagine. He furnished a philosophical reason to justify European enslavement of Africans, and more generally to justify European empire building in the Americas, Africa, and Asia. Hegel's false image of Africa celebrated the power and uniqueness of European consciousness. But what could be the motivation for the contemporary classicists' divorce of Africa from the world?

Divorcing Africa from the world provides Europeans a reason to believe that they owe nothing to Africans (or Asians and Native Americans) if Africans contributed nothing to European civilization's contemporary world-wide expressions. Hegel's philosophy forbade any connection between Africa and Egypt. His replicant philosophies would have us dissociate Africa from the rest of the world. His philosophy is best expressed in the claims of classicists who insist that Egyptians are not in any way Black Africans, and that there can be no foundational cultural connections between Egypt and Greece.

The neo-classicists come in many different stamps. Some would claim perfect genetic dissociation between Egypt and Africa (Bowersock, 7). Lefkowitz herself admits that the Greeks saw the Egyptians as "people of color": "Although the Greeks knew the Egyptians to be what we would now call "people of color," they did not think less or more or [sic] them (or any other Africans) on that account" (Lefkowitz, 1996, p. 13). But even this more moderate version of "neo-classicism" forbids any close cultural connections between Egypt and Greece.

Still, by acknowledging the African nature of Egyptian culture, Lefkowitz has herself taken great strides in the direction of a real Afrocentricity, not the false Afrocentricity that she demolishes so easily in her recent work. On one level, Afrocentricity is simply the collective name for the philosophical motivation to undertake research on Africa. This kind of research could not take place in academies under the influence of the anti-African sentiment rampant in the past century and in much of the present. But Africans on the continent and in the diaspora did not let the academies stop them from doing Afrocentric research in their own communities. As Lefkowitz makes clear, there are many versions of Afrocentricity. Many Afrocentrists, scholars and non-scholars alike, in and out of the academies, have jumped to apparently unjustifiable conclusions. But without the conviction that Afrocentric research is worth pursuing, the extraordinary discoveries that are now coming out of Africa could never have taken place.

Conclusion

A brief review of the consequences of Hegel's research program for African life may show why Afrocentrists undertake their research with a sense of urgency. Hegel claimed that the Africa beyond Egypt is the "dark of night," the "uncontrolled natural will" (Hegel, 1956, pp. 91, 104). Africans lack "the category of Universality" that naturally accompanies all) our [European] ideas" (93, my italics). Europeans, according to Hegel, simply can't understand Africans, because Africans can't think.

For Hegel, Egyptians stand in stark contrast to Africans. Herodotus' informants, he reminds us, "call the Egyptians the wisest of mankind" (Hegel, 1956, p. 204). Hegel professes to be stunned to find Egyptian intelligence, organizational power, and brilliant works of art—all "in the vicinity of African stupidity" (Hegel, 1956, p. 204). Amidst this barrage of anti-African racism, however, we find a striking passage that captures Hegel in astonishing self-contradiction.

 85

Hegel's environmental determinism made the Nile the prime mover of African culture, and Hegel speculates that African culture moved from South to North along the Nile: "With this is connected the consideration that Egypt probably received its culture from Ethiopia; principally from the island Meroe, which, according to recent hypotheses, was occupied by a sacerdotal people" (Hegel 1956, p. 201). Hegel makes this remark in an offhandedly, seemingly unconscious way, as if a "trick of reason" suddenly forced him to undercut his attempts to separate Egypt from the rest of Africa. We should hardly be surprised to find Egyptian enlightenment "in the vicinity of African stupidity," if Africans were in fact the source of Egyptian culture. Hegel's fully conscious racist philosophy would have halted the research that has turned his slip of the tongue into a legitimate research program. Respected archaeologists like Charles Bonnet (1990) and David O'Connor (1993) take seriously the hypothesis that Nubia, Hegel's Ethiopia, made important cultural contributions to the growth and development of early civil, cultural and social developments in Egypt.

Their discoveries have demonstrated Nubia's cultural autonomy and intercourse with Egypt and central Africa. Frank Yurco (1996) interprets a 6th dynasty tomb inscription (2330 B.C.E.) as evidence that Egyptians valued central African culture for its music and dancing seventeen hundred years prior to the Nubian conquest of Egypt. Frank Snowden (1996, 1983) emphasizes the ancient Greek belief that the Nubian was a most enlightened Egyptian dynasty. The results of this kind of research have accumulated to the point that an "Egypt in Africa" exhibit in Indianapolis can celebrate the demise of racist research guidelines disconnecting Egypt and Africa. But when one bad philosophy vanishes, others often take its place.

Contemporary classicists like Lefkowitz and Bowersock take up Hegel's old theme with a new twist. Their argument makes the ancient Greeks proto-Afrocentrists in the sense that Afrocentrists

 86

claim Egyptian foundations for Greek culture. As Bowersock puts it, the Greeks naively "supposed that they had borrowed from the Egyptians," but newfangled 20th century scholarship's analytical tools can prove the Afrocentric Greeks wrong. Bowersock follows Hegel in insisting that Egyptians can only be linked to Black Africans in a "simple-minded geographical sense...Ancient Egyptians did not consider themselves Africans or Blacks..." (Lefkowitz, 1996, p. 7).

As we saw above, Lefkowitz at least admits that the Greeks portrayed Egyptians as "what we would now call "people of color" (Lefkowitz, 1996, p. 13). In her view, the Egyptians had significant cultural ties to Africa beyond Egypt. She cites as examples semi-divine kingship in East Africa and "elaborate rhythmic hand-clapping at festivals, which Herodotus observed during his visit to Egypt..." (Lefkowitz, 1996, p. 135).

In attacking Hegel's disconnection of Egypt from Africa, however, Lefkowitz actually steps backwards into Hegel's arms. She repudiates Hegel's disconnection of Egypt from Africa but accentuates Egypt's separation from Greece. While admitting that Egyptians influenced Greeks "in various ways over along period of time" (Lefkowitz, 1996, p. 161), she insists that Egypt cannot be connected to Greece in any foundational way. In making Egypt African and separating Egypt from Greece, she reaffirms Hegel's conviction in a new way: Not out of Africa!

Philosophies like Hegel's have inspired Europeans to neglect research in the Africa out of Egypt for nearly two centuries. Bonnet (1996) contrasts the hordes of archaeologists working in Egypt with the ten now working in Nubia. If researchers believe that Africa contributed little to Greece by way of Egypt, they will hardly look for Africa's foundational contributions to non-Greek cultures right in Africa. Hegel and Lefkowitz's research philosophy would stop the investigation that will disclose a new "Egypt in Africa." It would also prevent research from moving beyond "Egypt in Africa" to explore "Africa in the World."

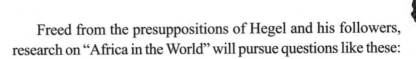
Freed from the presuppositions of Hegel and his followers, research on "Africa in the World" will pursue questions like these:

- Do great civilizations spring into being through immaculate conception or evolve gradually through cultural diffusion?
- Do modern cultures evolve from limited numbers of ancient cultures in the same way that modern humans seem to have evolved from small populations in Africa?
- Could the rest of Africa have given as much to Egypt through cultural diffusion as Egypt might have given to Greece?
- Did ancient Africans develop philosophies that may have been passed on to the rest of the world through Egyptian civilization?

Bonnet and O'Connor's work cited above and Erik Hornung's (1981) respected claims about the sophistication of ancient Egyptian ontology provide a scholarly impetus for pursuing these questions. Merritt Ruhlen (1991), Colin Renfrew (1994, 1992), and Luigi Cavalli-Sforza's (1991, 1981) work legitimizes "Out of Africa" research programs in linguistics and biology as well as archaeology. Afrocentrists are taking bold steps to help reverse "European consciousness'" long-standing efforts to make research serve racism. The Afrocentric research program distinctively models the uses of research against racism. Lefkowitz' convictions that Egyptians are what she would call "people of color," that Egypt is an African culture, and that the Greeks were influenced by the Egyptians over long periods of time in many ways show how much she has overcome Hegel's European racism. Lefkowitz' claim that she will always teach her students about the Afrocentric paradigm in the future shows the power of Afrocentricity in action—even in the minds of its most ardent critics. *Not Out of Africa* has helped bring Afrocentricity to the surface of American consciousness.

References

Bonnet, Charles (1990). *Kerma: royaume de Nubia*. Geneve: Museum d'Art et d'Histoire.

Bonnet, Charles (1996). *Who Were the Ancient Nubians?* Lecture, Smithsonian National Museum of African Art, March 2.

Bowersock, Glen (1996). *Rescuing the Greeks*. The New York Times Book Review, February 25, 6-7.

Cavalli-Sforza, Luigi Luca and Feldman, Marc W. (1981). *Cultural Transmission and Evolution: a Quantitative Approach*. Princeton: Princeton University Press.

Cavalli-Sforza, Luigi Luca (1991). *Genes, Peoples and Languages*. Scientific American, 265(5), 104-110.

Diop, Cheikh Anta (1992). *Civilization or Barbarism: An Authentic Anthropology*. Trans. Yaa-Lengi Meema Ngemi, orig. 1981) Brooklyn: Lawrence Hill Books.

Drake, St. Clair (1990). *Black Folk Here and There, 2 Vols*. Los Angeles: Center for Afro-American Studies, UCLA.

Hall, J. A. and I.C. Jarvie, eds(1992). World Languages and *Human Dispersals: A Minimalist View in Transition to Modernity: Essays on Power, Wealth and Belief*. Cambridge: Cambridge University Press.

Hegel, G.W.F. (1956). *The Philosophy of History* (J. Sibree, Trans.). New York: Dover.

89

Hornung, Erik (1982). *Conceptions of God in Ancient Egypt: The One and The Many* (J. Baines, trans., orig. 1971). Ithaca: Cornell University Press.

Lefkowitz, Mary (1996). Not Out of Africa.: *How Afrocentricity Became an Excuse to Teach Myth as History*. New York: Basic Books.

O'Connor, David (1993). *Ancient Nubia: Egypt's Rival in Africa*. Philadelphia: The University of Pennsylvania Museum of Archaeology and Anthropology.

Renfrew, Colin (1994). *World Linguistic Diversity*. Scientific American, (270(1), 116-123.

Ruhlen, Merrit (1991). *A guide to the World's Languages, Vol. 1: Classification With Postscript*. Stanford: Stanford University Press.

Snowden, Frank (1996). *Greco-Roman and Early Christian Views of Nubia and Nubians*. Lecture, Smithsonian National Museum of African Art, March 9.

Preserving the Eurosupremacist Myth
Don Luke, Ph.D.
San Diego City College

   This essay addresses the current phenomenon of Afrocentric-bashing by scholars like Mary Lefkowitz. I do not intend to address Lefkowitz's ignorance and lack of academic competence as she attempts to deny the African basis for Greek civilization. Others have and are performing that service quite adequately in this volume. On the other hand, it is my intention here to show how the Lefkowitz syndrome has been quite typical of hegemonic Eurocentric scholarship for the past three or four centuries. Lefkowitz and her ilk generally have no background in African people's history not only within the African continent itself, but also outside of the continent. What they often do is to demonstrate their arrogance by examining African issues within the context of their idea of Western conquest. Outside their continent, Africans have made significant contributions to other people's civilizations; but Eurocentric scholars like Lefkowitz display such a pronounced ignorance of this fact that they undermine their own academic credibility and competence. They attempt to deny that which they have insufficient knowledge.

   Even so, Lefkowitz is very clear about the need to defend the notion of Eurosupremacy. One need do no more than read the series of articles between her and Martin Bernal in the *Bryn Mawr Review,* of April and May 1996 to apprise themselves of this fact. Herein she arrogantly displays her ignorance. It is my purpose here to demonstrate that, far from being an aberration, the Lefkowitz syndrome has been typical of Eurosupremacist scholarship for the past few centuries. Despite their inability to competently critique Afrocentric scholarship, hegemonic Eurocentrists are dedicated to the task of maintaining the myth of Eurosupremacy. Classicists like Lefkowitz are not unique because Old Norse scholars, likewise, are unable to accept the fact that a significant part of that early culture came out of Africa.

The evidence from several fields including cultural anthropology, and the Old Norse sagas, themselves, demonstrate quite clearly that significant numbers of "true Negros" were present in ancient and medieval Scandinavia. Further investigation reveals that this presence is adamantly denied by the hegemonists due to their ignorance of African people's history, their inability to see beyond their self-imposed cultural restrictions, and/or their need to maintain the myth of Eurosupremacy. Not only were these Africans present, but they were also referred to, as Danes, and these Danes were arguably the most influential segment of the Scandinavian population during the Viking Age. Most Eurocentrists conceive of the African as static and "primitive." Thus the hegemonists have an artificial and contrived bias imposed upon their conception of the African's capabilities. To work from the premise of African cultural inferiority, relative to the Caucasian as a given, added to the notion of the impossibility of ancient African preeminence, prevents one from being able to accept evidence to the contrary.

Consequently, when an independent non-Indo European presence is discovered in early Europe, the African is automatically eliminated as the possible occupant. And among other possibilities (which includes anyone else), the most likely candidates are always some non-descript, unidentifiable quasi-Caucasoid type which makes its appearance from out of nowhere only to disappear without a trace once the particular episode which required their presence is past. The Atlantean construct relative to pre-dynastic majesty of the Nile Valley is one example. Others include the "Celt," "Ugrian," "Mediterranean," "Eastern," and "pre- Indo European Kurgan".

The one case where an African presence in early Europe can be accepted by these scholars is when that presence results from the actions of others. In this way, the sacred paradigm of African *stasis* is upheld, and no challenge to the Aryan Model of European cultural supremacy occurs (Bernal, 1987). The African captured

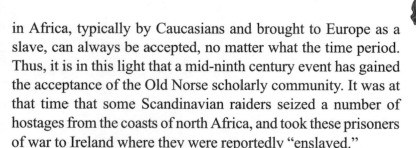

in Africa, typically by Caucasians and brought to Europe as a slave, can always be accepted, no matter what the time period. Thus, it is in this light that a mid-ninth century event has gained the acceptance of the Old Norse scholarly community. It was at that time that some Scandinavian raiders seized a number of hostages from the coasts of north Africa, and took these prisoners of war to Ireland where they were reportedly "enslaved."

Actual historical records show that Africans had a continuous self-initiated presence in northern Europe from ancient times through the Viking Age. Above all, it will be demonstrated below that the only way this information could be retrieved and correctly interpreted is by approaching the research findings from a non-hegemonic Eurocentric perspective.

A most important distinction between the research methodologies of the Africalogist and the hegemonic Eurocentric, concerns the matter of prescription and prediction. The Africalogist, unlike the Eurocentric scholar, is not guided by a need to prescribe and predict. Far too many Eurocentric scholars have attempted to maintain the axiom of the superiority of European culture over that of all others. There is a paradigm, formally established in the late eighteenth century, that the Indo-European is and always has been the most culturally advanced and "progressive" race among mankind (Bernal, 1987, 215-23). This paradigm serves to justify the international status quo for the past four centuries. Thus the Eurocentric approach to research is not only hegemonic, but it is also tied to extra-academic concerns that have a direct bearing on the outcome of that research.

These extra-academic concerns take priority over the academic ones, because the social status quo must be upheld at all costs. Eurocentric research is compromised from the start, and the outcome of such research is actually predictable. It is predictable because certain socio-cultural conclusions are prescribed: things European must always appear superior, and things African, inferior. This is where the *theory* takes *precedence*

over the evidence. If evidence is found which refutes the theoretical image of the African as the perennial static and "primitive," such evidence has to be re-interpreted and explained away so as not to undermine the sanctity of their theory of Eurosupremacy. Therefore ideology prevents objectivity. This is the Aryan Model noted by Bernal in *Black Athena*.

The Africalogist is unaffected by such extra-academic needs. S/he has no social system of Afrosupremacy to maintain, nor a social theory to protect. Theory never takes precedence over the evidence, but is in fact moderated by the evidence. If the evidence does not support the theory, it is the theory that has to be modified to fit the evidence. The Africalogist, therefore, is never afraid to discover the unexpected. There is no need to suppress "harmful" evidence and keep it from the light of day. On the contrary, their purpose is to liberate that information previously suppressed by the edicts of the Aryan Model.

While the hegemonist seeks to "predict and control," the Africalogist seeks to "interpret and understand" (Asante, 1987, 18). It is for this reason that the Afrocentric approach to research is currently the most effective means to open up one's understanding to the realities of African history, a major component of world history. That history has been verified by real life experience, and needs only to be accurately interpreted and understood; it has already happened, therefore it cannot be predicted, controlled or reshaped.

It is only those who fear the truth that oppose its exposure. Asante notes that, "social science in the West is imperialistic, (it is) the disciplinary justification for expansion" (Asante, 1983, 5). Obviously a non-hegemonic, anti-imperialistic approach to the social sciences is a direct challenge to Western scholarship. One's goal should be to reconstruct history, not to deconstruct it. The task, therefore, as Asante noted, is to "confront oppressive discourse" (Asante, 1990, ix), not to ignore it. Understandably, the methods and conclusions of Afrocentric scholars are often diametrically opposed to the European intellectual tradition (Asante, 1983, 10). Thus such findings as are presented herein will not always be welcomed from those who have supported the Eurocentric status quo. Nonetheless, it is the evidence and the recovery of the truth that is the major concern here, not the goodwill of those who have obscured and distorted this truth. It is the evidence, not one's pronouncements, that will be the final justification for one's efforts.

For the sake of clarity, therefore, it is necessary to re-emphasize a point noted above with regard to the detractors. In order to make meaningful statements about a people, one must first be adequately familiar with the history and culture of that people. If Western researchers, whether classicists like Mary Lefkowitz or in this case the Old Norse scholars, are to make meaningful statements about Africans, they must first be familiar with African history and culture. They must be familiar with *all* of African history as *African* history. They must be sufficiently aware of African culture to notice its indices *wherever* they appear. They must understand that the African is defined in terms of his own history and culture, not by someone else's arbitrary and irrelevant criteria. But above all, they must possess the necessary integrity and honesty, free of ideological bias, to be able to acknowledge these realities.

The Western scholars, which include the Old Norse scholars, have shown themselves to be extremely lacking with reference to all of the above. African people have a history in their own right, not one which is an appendage to European history, but one that antedates all other histories. Africans are therefore defined by their own traditions, not by that of their temporary usurpers to the research. As C.T. Keto notes, the Africa centered perspective of history rests on the premise that it is valid to posit Africa as a geographical and cultural starting base in the study of peoples of African descent. This perspective makes it easier to trace and understand *social patterns* of their existence, the *institutional*

patterns of their *actions,* and the intellectual patterns of their thoughts *within the changing context of time [and place* (emphasis is mine)] (Keto, 1989, 1).

When dealing with the African in this sense, one comes to understand that there are certain basic cultural patterns among African peoples that persist over time and space. Diop has made this point quite clear in his *Cultural Unity.* Thus, even when the scientist finds communities of Africans in Europe, the people in these communities will continue to exemplify certain cultural practices which are at variance with those of the local Indo-Europeans, and which identify them, unmistakably, as Africans. This same cultural tenacity, as Diop has shown, applies to the Indo-European when he relocates to Africa, for instance. Thus cultural indices are a type of "fingerprint" which follows and helps to identify a people wherever they go. So when the early Danes exemplify a tendency toward agriculture, and the practice of inhumation in stark contrast to the Swedish and Norwegian tendency to herding and cremation (Sturluson, 1991,3-4; Simpson, 1980, 30, 41), we could be witnessing the northern cradle - southern cradle dichotomy that Diop wrote of. This possibility is strengthened when one considers the even more pronounced dichotomy between the Vanir and the Aesir, perhaps the prototypes of the early Danish vs. Norwegian and Swedish types respectively.

This article does not argue for the presence of Blacks in medieval Scandinavia. That significant numbers of "Black" or "swarthy" people were present in medieval Scandinavia is a matter of record. The Old Norse sagas testify to their extensive presence. The object of this present work is to demonstrate by example the tactics taken by Old Norse scholars (which are the same tactics used by "classicists," etc.) as they attempt to deny the identity of the Black people of early Europe as being Africans, i.e., "Negroes." Before pursuing the issue of physical appearance, one must consult the historical record to see if there is a basis for an African ("true Negro") presence in early Scandinavia. Our

Old Norse scholars, like other Eurosupremacists, show a marked ignorance about the history of African people, therefore a cursory review of the African presence in early Europe would be instructive.

Inside the field of Old Norse studies, one would find a work by Snorri Sturluson (1179-1241). He was one of the chief Old Icelandic saga compilers during the age when these family histories were being set down in writing. He tells us while describing the interior of Russia that Africans or *blamenn* were residing in that northern European territory. This reference is too close to home and may lead one to suspect that the Black people of next door Scandinavia may also be "Negroes," so characteristically Hermann Palsson and Paul Edwards, two of the most published and well known scholars in the field dispute Sturluson's statements regarding the presence of Africans (Palsson and Edwards, 1989, 28). This is the same tactic used by Ms Lefkowitz in *Not Out of Africa* as she attempts to challenge the veracity of the statements made by Greek scholars regarding Africa's cultural influence on Greece. The modern day scholars will even reject their own authorities in order to perpetuate the myth of Eurosupremacy.

Outside of Sturluson's reference, there is much solid evidence which places Africans in early Scandinavia from the second millennium B.C.E. and before, down through the Viking Age. Diop's "Origin of the Ancient Egyptians," *Unesco General history of Africa,* vol. II: 27-57 (1981), and Asa Hilliard's "Royal Images of Ancient Kemet," *Free Your Mind:* Return to the *Source - African* origins film slide presentation [1986-7] clearly establish the "true Negro" identity of the ancient Kamites. The Eurocentric world of Egyptology has presented no concrete evidence to dispute either of these materials because there is no evidence to dispute them. We begin, therefore, with the fact that the ancient Kamites were Black Africans.

97

The ancient trading routes of the Nile Valley Africans included one branch that began on the coasts of Kemet, extended to the west through the Mediterranean, and northward along the coast of western Europe into the Baltic Sea. Archaeologists A. H. Sayce and H. R. Hall, in the *Journal of Egyptian Archeology,* vol. I. both report on this route which linked the Nile Valley to western Europe, especially the British Isles and Scandinavia. Africans retrieved amber from the Baltic, according to some archaeological finds, as early as the Sixth Dynasty (Rice, 1980, 32).

In *The Great Pyramid: Its Divine Message*, Davidson and Aldersmith elaborate on the findings of Sayce and Hall. First speaking on the subject of megalithic (huge stone) structures, they note "Brittany lies on the Southern track of the megalithic builders . . . The circles and alignments of North-Western Europe lie on the Northern track of the megalithic builders from Western Asia and Egypt". The attempt to include the Phoenicians, who later became sailing partners with the Kamites, as megalithic builders, has no historical verification. This is another example of attempting to downplay the achievements of the Africans by including an alleged "mid-eastern" element with their achievements. It is true that these African colonists who lived in southwest Asia did later (around the mid second millennium) join their kinsmen as sailing partners and as agents. But the Phoenicians were never known as great builders. And the legends of the British Isles clearly identify Africans as the builders of the great megalithic structures like Stonehenge (Geoffrey of Monmouth, 1958, 164-5).

Moreover, as Davidson and Aldersmith add, not only did the erection of these huge monuments along the coasts of Europe follow a sea route, but "This undoubtedly points to the fact that these monuments were erected near colonized ports of call." In other words, Africans were establishing colonies all along the western European coasts. These archaeological findings are in accord with the historical records which tell us that "during the reign of Tuthmosis III (circa - 1500), the dominion of Egypt extended ... from Nubia to Northern Asia". But Senusert I of the Twelfth Dynasty (circa -1900) had already included "a great part of Europe in his conquest" (James, 1976, 11).

Who else but a colony of Africans around the Baltic could have influenced the Suebian Germans to worship the African goddess, Aset, as reported by Tacitus at the end of the first century? Who else but a colony (permanent residents) would build elaborate burial structures for their *inhumed* dead all over northern Europe, especially in Denmark? Such was the practice of the Vanir of old Scandinavian mythology, and the Beaker People of anthropology, who were the probable fore-bearers of the early African Danes, whose Southern Cradle culture was in stark contrast to the later arriving Indo-Europeans. And further, anthropologist Roland Dixon reports that during this same period of time, the skeletal remains from Mecklenburg, Germany, on the Baltic coasts were primarily "Proto-Australoid and Proto-Negroid" [Blacks] (Dixon, 1923, 74-5). So much for northern European Teutonic purity.

During the Viking Age, the Norwegian raiders were referred to as the White Foreigners by the Irish, Welsh and Scots. The Danish invaders were referred to as the Black Foreigners. Martin Bernal says the root "Dan-" and the names it forms can be traced back to ancient Kemet and the area surrounding the Mediterranean. If these origins are in Kemet, the term would have passed into the languages in the surrounding areas. At any rate Danaos, the twin brother of Egyptos, was the progenitor of the Danaids who travelled to Greece and later moved further north and west into Europe where they were known as the Danaans/ Dananns. Whether some of these became connected with the Dark Elves of Irish mythology as some have suggested (MacKenzie, W. C., n.d., 46-51), or not, the Danaans like the Pelasgians of early Greece were certainly not of the same culture or stock as the Dorians (Aryans). Even Bernal, who is certainly not an Afrocentrist, tends to suggest this.

Both brothers, Danaos and Egyptos, and the Danaids are explicitly described as being "Black". It is not certain that the *early* Danes of Scandinavia were Danaids. But that the early Danes were Black like the Danaids is clear. And that their culture was similar to the Danaids but differed in certain significant aspects from the Teutonic Swedes and Norwegians is also clear.

For those who find it difficult to reconcile the idea of Africans dwelling in the cool climate of northern Europe, they need to consult the early climatic record of Scandinavia. Between –8000 B.C. and 5000 B.C., the average summer temperatures in Scandinavia were about twenty degrees warmer than they are today (Oakley, 1972, pp. 18-23). And after 5000 B.C., the winters became even milder and the summers more humid. Human remains as late as the Bronze Age, when the (Kemetic) phallic-like symbolism of a Southern "fertility cult" abounded in the area, show that during this period people were scantily dressed. Another author provides a more detailed description:

> "We notice the men wore a garment round their hips held in place by a leather belt. This garment sometimes extended right up under the arm-pits and *the cut occasionally bears a resemblance to certain Egyptian* costumes . . . The arms and legs were bare. Leather sandals were known. A woman wore a blouse with half-length sleeves, cut exactly like blouses of the present day . . . *Bronze age girls also sometimes wore the cord skirt and nothing else,* just bare legs and a bare top. It may sound peculiar, for the Danish climate hardly seems appropriate for such flimsy wear. But the weather during the bronze age was much warmer than it is today; it was drier, *summer practically the whole year round . . .* " [italics are mine].
>
> (Lauring, 1991, 30-1)

"Preserving the Eurosupremacist Myth"
Don Luke, Ph.D.
San Diego City College

The Bronze Age in Scandinavia seemed to appear contemporaneous with the imperial age of the Eighteenth Dynasty of Ancient Kemet which was noted above. Hall and Sayce noted that "blue glass beads" which originated from the latter part of the Eighteenth Dynasty and the early part of the Nineteenth Dynasty "are met with plentifully in the *Early Bronze Age* tumuli of Wiltshire *in association with* amber *beads* [italics are mine]. Sayce continues, "amber was carried at an early date from the Baltic to Britain and the gold of Ireland was conveyed to Scandinavia" (18). And according to researchers in the field, there were no Germanic tribes or any other "Indo-Europeans" cultures in Scandinavia during *the early Bronze Age.* These Caucasian tribes arrived sometime after -1000 (Loyn, 1977, 10; Derry, 1979, 7).

The northern areas enjoyed a comparatively mild climate, even mild for sailing and exploring right through the Viking Age and up to approximately 1200. After this the climate grew progressively colder and harsher, gradually becoming what it is today. By the middle of the fifteenth century, glaciers began to advance across Greenland (Jones, 1968, 307). Medieval Scandinavia was in fact very different from today's Scandinavia, both in climate and population make-up. Projecting the present back into the past lends plausibility to the Aryan Model, without which it cannot work. Our Old Norse establishment and other Eurosupremacists like Mary Lefkowitz are literally living in a fantastic past of their own creation.

On the other hand, what is the basis for the notion that Africans cannot function in northern climates? This author has been told by more than one native Scandinavian that, due to the warm current of the Gulf Stream, the winters in Reykjavik, Iceland are not quite as harsh as those in Ithaca, New York. Why is it then that so many people find it inconceivable that Africans could live and flourish in medieval Iceland, Southwest Norway or Zealand, but don't give a second thought to the fact that thousands of Africans have functioned for the past few centuries in central New York

State where Ithaca is located, and even in upper New York State, or in Canada?

Furthermore, recall that it was a Black African general, Hannibal Barca, who with thousands of African soldiers, many of whom were able to survive the falling snow, frigid temperatures, inhospitable terrain of the Alps, and the savage attacks of the "primitive" European tribes which lined their route to Rome. What then is incomprehensible about African Vikings waging formidable campaigns against their adversaries in northern and western Europe? There is nothing unusual about it unless one's mind is imprisoned in the Aryan Model. The whole world has changed in the past 500 years, in more ways than one; and most of us are only now beginning to realize the full extent of this fact.

After establishing some historical background, we can return to the issue of physical appearance and color agnomens. The Old Norse establishment insists that color terms like "swarthy" and "Black" designated a person's (Caucasian) hair color, not their complexion. With reference to my inquiries, I received the following responses on the subject:

"Although I am not a physical anthropologist, 1 believe I can answer *your question with some certainty. 1 have never heard* of any serious modern scientific claims that "Proto-Negroid" or "Proto-Australoid" skeletal material has been identified from the prehistoric period in Northern Europe." Dr. Noel D. Broadbent, Program Director National Science Foundation, Washington, D.C. (July 2, 1990).

"There is no archeological evidence to support your theory that Africans were among the earliest inhabitants of Denmark . . ." John Lund, National Museum of Denmark Department of Near Eastern and Classical Antiquities (April 24, 1990). *"As a matter of fact, there is no evidence whatsoever* of "Black people (Negroes)" living in early Iceland or Scandinavia. On the other

hand, the Sagas often describe some people as being "Black" or "light", "red", even "White" *which simply indicates that they were dark-haired, fair-haired or blond, even albinos.* Secondly, the original inhabitants of northern Scandinavia were *most likely related* to the dark-haired Lapps, . . ." Arni Bjbrnsson, Ethnological Curator National Museum of Iceland (May 9, 1990).

In fact, while presenting his analysis of *The Journal of African Civilizations,* vol. 7, #2, Paul Edwards said, "One has to watch out for color words in languages not one's own, a particular problem arises in the interpretation of the words "Black" in Old Norse . . . Don Luke's essay on the African presence in early times in Britain and Scandinavia is particularly guilty of misrepresentation . . ." (Edwards, 1987, 403).

Edwards goes on to say, referring to the term *svarti* (swarthy), "This is translated loosely as "Black," sometimes "swarthy," but is not used for Black African complexions, and normally, as in the earlier examples, refers to the color of hair" (Edwards, 404). He then goes on to say that I and other authors in that particular issue "persistently pervert a language of which they clearly have no knowledge in an attempt to demonstrate African origins". If what Professor Edwards and others say is true with reference to Black agnomens, we would ask them to explain why Africans (blamenn, "Negroes") are referred to in several passages in the Old Norse literature as being "swarthy/Black."

In "Sorli saga sterka," some blamenn are described as swarthy: svartir, but with no hair on their heads: "ekkert her a *hofdi.* " And in *Barlaams ok Josapha rs Saga,* there is a passage which Fritzner says was particularly used for "Negros" and Ethiopians during the saga writing period, *"blamenn skipti sinu svarta skinni . . . "*: "though an African ("Negro") changes his swarthy skin . . . " (Keyser and Unger, 1851, 169). We would ask if Mr. Edwards and others are not intentionally perverting a language of which they do have some knowledge of? Moreover, they must certainly be aware of the fact that when the hair color of an individual is being referred to in the Old Icelandic language, the color term is usually followed by the words "a har" (of hair). On the other hand, based on one's perspective, s/he can accept or reject the evidence for what it is.

For one to argue that "swarthy denotes hair color and is not used for *Black African* complexions," would seem to indicate not only one's lack of understanding of the basic lexicons, but also a lack of familiarity with the primary material. And neither of these possibilities would apply to Paul Edwards. So why does he make these statements? Based on the primary materials, one, hair color does not typically figure in "swarthiness," and two, the term *does* typically describe "Black African" complexions. Other examples confuting Mr. Edwards' statements include the following. There is Viga-Glum, the eponymous character of a saga who is described as swarthy *(skolbrunn),* yet has White hair, *hvitr a* har! Could his description account for one scholar's attempt to re-define the word *skolbrunn* as "joined brows" in the footnotes of one edition (Kristjansson, 1956, 15) in order to avoid the contradiction? And in *Eyerbyggja Saga,* Arngrimr Thorgrimsson is also described as *swarthy* but with *light-reddish hair.* Palsson and Edwards did a translation of this saga, but unlike Paul Schach who also did an English translation, the former conveniently left out the mention of Arngrimur's swarthiness in their edition. This might be another example of re-adjusting the evidence to maintain an unworkable theory. So once again, who is perverting the language?

Based on the foregoing evidence, it appears that many of the scholars within the discipline of Old Norse Studies (as are Ms Lefkowitz and many classicists) are trapped within the Aryan Model and its narrow frame of reference. Their conclusions relative to the human populations of early Scandinavia are derived from fabricated paradigms growing out of premises which are clearly false. To repeat, it has been demonstrated from the examples brought forth above, that Eurosupremacist scholarship will reject evidence from their own primary sources when such evidence refutes the cherished theories of European cultural and racial hegemony. The founders of the Aryan Model were never actually interested in the truth, but only in the creation and preservation of a myth.

In attempts to disassociate the Old Norse proper name, *Sverting(r)* from the modern common noun, *svertingi* ("Negro"), the scholars constantly stress the fact that *Svertingr* was *merely a* person's name, while *svertingi* defines a type of person. It is as if *Svertingr* had no meaning in itself. But no name, even proper names, are *merely* names. They all have meanings. For example, after surnames came into being in England, *Blackman* was a surname for a Black man [a "Negro"] (Smith, 43). And as Magnusson (1989, 999) points out, both "svertingi . . . og [and] Sverting(u)r" are derived from the same term, "sverta kv. 'svart litarefni'" (Black pigment). Thus *svertingis* and *Svertingrs* are both Black pigmented people, i.e., people of Black complexion. That the two words are identical in meaning is further confirmed by both Holthausen (291, 292) and DeVries (565, 568) who show that, in Old Icelandic, the surname *Svertingr* was an alternate term for "svartr," i.e., "the Black." And "the Black" was a term used in the Old Norse sagas to designate people who were phenotypically "true Negros" (as in the case of Thorstein the Black, below).

Likewise, in Modern Icelandic, "the Black" is a label used to refer to a "true Negro": *blokkumanna [svertingi)* (Sorenson, 1080 under "the"). And Gwyn Jones notes that the color names assigned to people during the Viking Age were personally descriptive (Jones, 1964, 68). Just as *Svart,* the son of L11f Aurogodi was a personal name for a man who was *a svarri,* so *Sverting,* Svart's great-grandson, was a personal name for a man who was a *sverting-i* (Black-skinned man) In a similar fashion, *Skarphe3inn* was a personal name for a *skarpleitr* (sharp-faced man).

In Old Norse, one synonym given for *svartr,* a swarthy man, is *sverting-r* (Holthausen, 291; De Vries, 565). Another synonym for *svartr* is *svertingi* ["Negro"] (Johannesson, 1956, 808). If a "Negro" was a svartr *mar,* and a svartr *mar* was a sverting, then clearly a "Negro" was a *sverting* in the early period. Thus the *Svertingrs* of the Sagas and the *svertingis* of modern times are one and the same people, phenotypically. But that the term applied to any other non "Negro" group, or was used *explicitly* to include Caucasian Scandinavians has yet to be demonstrated by the detractors. To this researcher's knowledge, and based on the evidence presented above and below, *the only distinct phenotype that is explicitly, routinely and consistently identified/described as "swarthy" in the Old Norse Sagas, in those cases where such an explicit identification is actually made, is the blama3r or "Negro" (African).* Again, it rests with the hegemonic Eurocentrists to demonstrate, *with* examples from the *primary sources,* the clear and *explicit* identification of any other (racial) phenotype distinct from the "Negro" (including those with an identifiable "Negro" lineage) that is routinely and consistently referred to as "swarthy."

Without such evidential verification to the contrary, these Eurocentric scholars are merely working on an *assumption, a theory, or* an axiom. It is clear that a White-skinned Caucasoid phenotype or *hvitr mar* cannot, at the same time, be a "blue-skinned" "Negro" phenotype or *svartr mar:* The two types are *distinctly* different, phenotypically, as demonstrated in the *Fornmanna Sogur,* vol. III, 189 and vol. X, 420, just to mention two examples (see below). Thus the possibility of a Caucasian being a *svartr mar* or *sverting* is eliminated.

But the interpretation of any evidence is largely predetermined by the premises from which one proceeds. If one proceeds from the premise that there were and could not have been any resident

Africans in medieval Scandinavia, then it logically follows that *Svertingr* could not have had any reference to "true Negros." If, on the other hand, one proceeds from the premise that Africans were residing in and around northern Europe, then *Svertingr* would have had reference to "Negros."

And judging from the available evidence, it appears highly unlikely that those individuals who were referred to as "swarthy" or "Black" during the medieval period were not "Negros," or at least "Negros" in mixture. To those who argue that the term *swarthy* does not necessarily imply an African lineage, one responds by saying that, in addition to the African, himself, the word *swarthy* was/is used to identify those alleged Caucasians within the European world who display outward indications of a "Negroid" ancestry. This ancestry is evident primarily through a "colored" complexion, even if this complexion is no more than tawny. Such a complexion often accompanies the Black hair, but other Africoid physical traits may also be evident even as they are on some "Caucasians" of light coloring. A passing reference to well-known Europeans who were labelled as "swarthy" during their time, cross-referenced with such individuals from the literature of medieval Europe, will serve to verify this point.

Jean Baptiste Bernadotte, Charles XIV of Sweden and Norway, an alleged Caucasian, was described as "swarthy with wooly hair" (Rogers, 1970, 34). However, "the Moorish ancestry of his mother is a matter of local knowledge . . . there is very much of the *Negro* in his face," and he looked like "a mulatto" (Rogers, 34). Further, one of Bernadotte's daughters "was so dark that she was called "La Negresse" [Rogers quotes from sources contemporary to the subjects].

Ludwig van Beethoven, renowned composer, was described as being swarthy, "Blackish-brown complexion" (Rogers, 1970, 19). Beethoven's swarthiness, however, was not disassociated from his "Negroid" features: "Frederick Hertz, German anthropologist, in 'Race and Civilization,' refers twice to Beethoven's

'*Negroid* traits' and his 'dark' skin, and 'flat, thick nose'" (Rogers, 19). Beethoven was called "The Black Spaniard" (Rogers, 4).

Franz Joseph Haydn, Beethoven's contemporary, also swarthy, was called "The Moor" and a *"Blackamoor"* ["Negro"] (19). Charles II, King of England, who was referred to by such labels as "Black Boy" (Harvey, 1976, 20), and as possessing "unaesthetic swarthiness" (Bingham, 1976, 103), was descended from the Medici line whose Africoid strain was most evident in the faces of several of its noblemen (Rogers, 1967, 163-4). From this line also, was Alessandro dei Medici, Duke of Florence. The swarthy Alessandro, who had "a dark skin, thick lips, and wooly hair, . . . *was a mulatto"* (Rogers, 164).

Ludovico, Duke of Milan and member of the powerful Sforza family, had "very swarthy skin," but he also looked like "The Moor" ["Negro"] (Rogers, 164). Since Italians generally have dark or Black hair, it is obvious that hair color did not determine Ludovico's "swarthiness." Benedict de Spinoza, the seventeenth century philosopher and Portuguese-Spanish Jew, and Karl Marx, the nineteenth century German Jew, were both labelled "swarthy," and both just as surely display the frizzly hair, complexion and facial features *of the mulatto.* In fact, Marx was referred to as "The Moor" (Welling, 1991, 224). The Africoid component within the Jewish/Semitic populations is too well documented and discussed to merit the additional space here.

Speaking of the medieval European Jews, who were apparently more Africoid in appearance then than they are today, Merimee's novella, *Carmen,* acknowledges this reality. With regard to physical appearance, the narrator queries whether *Carmen is a Blackamoor (a Muslim] or a Jew.* And in Walter Scott's *Ivanhoe,* there is the swarthy Reuben, a "dark-browed and Black-bearded Israelite" (Scott, 1984, 122), and the young "Jewess," Rebecca, who had a "dark complexion" and Black hair "arranged in its own *little spiral of twisted* curls" [sveipr a harinu] (82).

"Preserving the Eurosupremacist Myth"
Don Luke, Ph.D.
San Diego City College

Among the Caucasoid populations of the recent centuries, a tawny complexion is sometimes referred to as "dark" or "swarthy." Under this standard, persons like Count Munck von Fulkila and Gustavus IV, whose photographs clearly depict light or tawny skinned individuals (Rogers, 1967, 193), could be described as "dark" by their White-skinned contemporaries. From the readings (Rogers, 194-5), it would appear, and not only in this present example, that such typically Africoid traits as full lips, broad or flat noses, prognathism, and frizzly or kinky hair tend to contribute to the "darkening" of a tawny-colored individual in the eyes of their Caucasian peers. Even so, one seems to be brought back to an inescapable conclusion.

That conclusion is that no matter what the actual hue, terms like "swarthy," "dark," and of course, "Black" appear to be used by Caucasians, both past and present, to designate both Africans and other "Caucasians," whose physical appearance, beginning with a "colored" complexion, reveal a recognizable amount of African ancestry. In fact, during the 1920s the Western social scientists determined that "three of the most important 'Negroid' traits [were]— 'swarthy skin, frizzly hair, and heavy features'" (Williamson, 1980, 126). And now for these same twentieth century Western scholars to look at medieval records and declare that those people, who are *described in these identical terms* as possessing these same features, could not be "Negros," is the worst kind of doublespeak. Not only is this an exercise in self-contradiction, but it is an insult to the intelligence of their readers.

The preceding descriptions of "Black" and "swarthy" Europeans, who turn out to be "Negros" and mulattos, are identical to those physical descriptions of "Black" and "swarthy" individuals which are found in the Old Norse sagas, as will be demonstrated below. The modern usage of the terms is so loose that it is sometimes applied to a Caucasian who has a suntan. As is the case with so many words, they tend to lose some of their original meaning over the centuries. This recent usage of the term, however, must be recognized for what it is, a recent development. It must not be projected back upon an earlier age in order to confuse and mislead. This has been done by many of our modern scholars.

Concerning the classic description of "Black skin and wooly curled hair," which is how the Scandinavians, themselves, define a "Negro": "möck hy, ulligt, krusigt har" (Svenska Akademien, 435), there are a number of individuals within the sagas who are described as such, and the following three will be presented as evidence of an African presence in medieval Iceland. From Chapter 63 *of Laxdaela Saga* are found two of these descriptions. First, there is Lambi Thorbjarnarson: *"skolbrunn mjok, svartr a har ok skrufharr"* ("very swarthy with Black wooly hair"). Next there is Thorstein svartr (Thorstein swarthy or Thorstein *the Black): "dokkjarpr a har ok hrokk mjok"* ("very wooly dark-brown hair"). Finally, there is a King Eystein in volume X of the *Fornmanna Sogur,* p. 420 who is described thus: "var svartr ok skrufharr" ("he was Black-skinned and wooly-haired"). *Skrufharr* and *hrokkinn* har are two terms for the same kind of hair (Sveinsson, 1934, 188 note 4; Bodvarsson, 605). *Skrufharr* is literally "screw-hair," or "spiral-hair" as in the case of *skrufstigi,* a spiral staircase. And *hrokkinn har,* is defined in the Icelandic lexicon literally as "wooly hair": *"ullha?rdur"* (Sorenson, 1984, 1224).

So there is no basis for confusion about either the type of hair or the racial lineage being referred to here. But Hermann Palsson, in a personal letter (May 2, 1991) assured this author that, "The terms *svartr* and *inn svarri* in the sagas refer to the colour of the hair and have absolutely no racial significance." And Paul Edwards, in another personal letter (July 25, 1990), said, "Readers of Old Icelandic texts in translation are often misled by the translation of 'Svarti' as 'Black'. In racial terms, a Black skin in Old Icelandic is *invariably 'Bla'* as in 'Blamann', 'Blamadr',

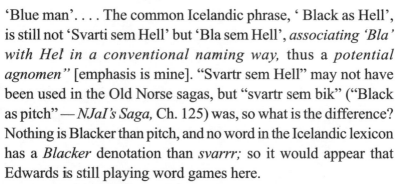

'Blue man'. . . . The common Icelandic phrase, ' Black as Hell', is still not 'Svarti sem Hell' but 'Bla sem Hell', *associating 'Bla' with Hel in a conventional naming way,* thus a *potential agnomen"* [emphasis is mine]. "Svartr sem Hell" may not have been used in the Old Norse sagas, but "svartr sem bik" ("Black as pitch" — *NJaI's Saga,* Ch. 125) was, so what is the difference? Nothing is Blacker than pitch, and no word in the Icelandic lexicon has a *Blacker* denotation than *svarrr;* so it would appear that Edwards is still playing word games here.

Black skin and blue skin were identical in Old Norse. In the Old Icelandic sagas, there is a character named Blaeng Stasson. Blaaeng the blue-skinned man was the son of Soti (sooty) the Black-skinned man. Even Paul Edwards was forced to concede that *svartr* was used to describe *blue skins,* but says "northern" blue skins were distinct from "southern" (African) blue skins [July 25, 1990 letter]. Falk and Torp define the "blue skin" of the blamadr as *"skinnende sort ": svartr* skin (S 8), and Grim Kveldulfsson of *Egil's* Saga is described as *"sort and styg":* swarthy and ugly (Petersen, 56).

Could there be any mystery as to why Egil Skallagrimsson of *Egil's Saga* has to be classified as White, despite the unmistakable evidence presented in his saga concerning his and others' physical descriptions? Besides being dark/grim of aspect, "mark of Aasyn som Fa~eren" (Petersen, 1901, 97), Egil was, likewise, swarthy, *"Egill var . . . skolbrunn"* (Ch. S 5), he was broad-nosed and thick-lipped: "Egil's features were strongly marked . . . a nose not long but very wide, lips broad and full" (Fell, 1975, 84). So Egil, an alleged "northern" blueman, is described with the identical terms that the Scandinavian scholars, themselves, use to define a "Negro": *"mork* (stundom chokladbrun [skolbrúnn]) *hy, . . . , bred, plats nasa o. tjocka lappar"* (Svenska Akademien, 435).

So, *according* to the *Scandinavians' own criteria, Egil Skallagrimsson looked like a dark-skinned "Negro"* or blamad~r.

But understanding the needs of Eurocentrists, must one wonder at the ridiculous White-skinned caricature painted by a seventeenth century European to represent Egil, and pictured on the front covers of Pálsson and Edwards' edition, and that of Christine Fell? This is the same mentality possessed by Ms. Lefkowitz who presumes to declare the testimony of the Greek and Roman historians invalid, concerning the African origin of Greek science, philosophy, etc.

Many translators seemingly ignorant of the variety of physical types among African peoples, whether mixed or unmixed, imprecisely translate certain physically descriptive terms assuming these terms could only apply to a Caucasian. Here is an illustration to show what happens when one proceeds from such a false assumption; they will mis-translate a word like *skrufharr* to merely mean "curly" hair. From the *Sturlunga Saga* we have, *"Hann var ma3r skrofhxrdr ok freknottr mjok"* ["He was a very freckled man with close-curled wooly hair"] (Jonsson, 1954).

Next follows a passage from *The Autobiography of Malcolm X* to show that one cannot take a Caucasian identity for granted while reading such descriptions: "He was a light, kind of *red-complexioned Negro,* as I was; about my height, and he had freckles" [emphasis mine] (153). The passage from *Malcolm X* reminds us of two things, one is a fact and the other is an obligation.

The fact is noted by the biologist, J. H. Lewis, and recounted by Frank Snowden: *'The hair of the Negra is more characteristic than is the color of* the skin; . . . no race other than the Negro *or one intermixed* therewith has *wooly or kinky* hair as a stable feature" (Snowden, 265). Even a hegemonic Eurocentric anthropologist like Hooten, describes the African's hair as matted and *wiry,* growing in *spirals.* Snowden adds that the western anthropologists have designated the "true Negro" as having *"tightly curled"* and *wiry* hair described as *wooly, frizzly,* or *kinky"* (8). So when one reads that another King Eystein was a handsome

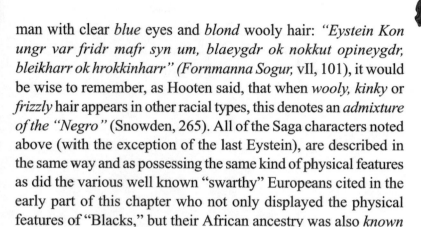

man with clear *blue* eyes and *blond* wooly hair: *"Eystein Kon ungr var fridr mafr syn um, blaeygdr ok nokkut opineygdr, bleikharr ok hrokkinharr" (Fornmanna Sogur,* vIl, 101), it would be wise to remember, as Hooten said, that when *wooly, kinky* or *frizzly* hair appears in other racial types, this denotes an *admixture of the "Negro"* (Snowden, 265). All of the Saga characters noted above (with the exception of the last Eystein), are described in the same way and as possessing the same kind of physical features as did the various well known "swarthy" Europeans cited in the early part of this chapter who not only displayed the physical features of "Blacks," but their African ancestry was also *known as a matter of fact.*

Concerning the obligation, referring to the Malcolm X quote, Afrocentrists must begin to challenge the unsubstantiated assumptions by the Old Norse scholars that people like Eric the Red (Eirik inn raudi) who bore the title of "the red" *(raudr, raudi)* were red-headed Caucasians. This author has seen no evidence to show that *raudi* refers to *raudha?rdr* (red-headed), as opposed to *raudleitr* (red-complexioned, ruddy). Moreover all the presumptions about Eric the Red's red hair are just that, presumptions. There is no physical description of Erlc in the *Grænlendinga Sogur* or in any other saga that I have seen. In fact, "many scholars believe that there must have been a lost *Eirik's Saga* which told the story of Eirik's life more fully" (Magnusson and Palsson, 1965, 49). Thus, the proposal made by some that Eric could have been a "red Negro," like Malcolm X, is no more absurd than the *presumption* that he was a red-haired Caucasian.

In fact, another *red* individual *(raudi, raudleitr),* Svein, was mentioned in Chapter 63 of *L.axdaela Saga.* Svein the *red* was the brother of Hunbogi *the dark* or *Black (dokklitar~r).* Jonsson defines *blar* (blue), svarrr (Black), and dokkr (dark) as all being interchangeable terms in the Old Icelandic lexicon *(Eddulyklar,* 1954, 77). It is also important to note that *dokkr* is also used to define the complexion of the medieval Blackamoors, whom

 113

the Old Icelandic lexicon clearly identifies as "Negros." In fact, even in Modern Icelandic the Blackamoor is still defined as a *"~eldokkur* ma~ur" [dark skinned man] (SigurD~sson, 1983, 893).

Moreover, that red hair and freckles alone did not entitle the bearer to be nicknamed "the red" is further proven by the fact that none of the prominent characters (presumably Caucasian) in the Old Icelandic family sagas who were described as having red hair and freckles, *alone,* were referred to as "the red." One case in point concerns Thrand, the central figure in the Faroe Islanders' Saga.

Another is Grettir of *Grettir's Saga,* who is never referred to as Grettir the Red but only as Grettir the Strong. And although Thrand was not referred to as "the red," another character in the Faroe Islanders' Saga was so fabled. One should remember also that, before moving to Iceland, Eric and his family came from Danish southwest Norway, the same area where men like Geirmund *Helskin,* and Earl *Soti (sooty* complexion) and his brother King Sulki ruled *(Grettir's* Saga, Ch. 2). Also, Eric the Red's long time friend and partner was a "northern" blue man or Black man, Thorhall svartr, whose physical description and character were identical to those of the "troll-like" "southern" blamenn berserkrs of the fictional sagas. This researcher is not declaring anything final here regarding the racial identity of Eric the Red. But what he is saying, however, is that based on the available evidence, and considering the information presented in this study, Eric's presumed Caucasian identity can no longer be accepted as a given because this is not supported by the evidence. It is only supported by our latter day Aryan establishment.

The practice of referring to a foreign African with a distinct title from a native "Negro" was no different in medieval European countries than it is in those countries today or in the United States. In Modern Icelandic, an African from the continent is an *Afrikuma3ur,* yet a "Negro" is still most commonly referred to as a *svertingi* (Black man). Given the extremely conservative nature of Icelandic traditions, it does not follow that the modern Icelanders' reference to "Negros" as *Blacks* (svartur), rather than as *Africans,* would be any different from the Saga writers' reference to *native* "Negros" as *svartrs* distinct from the foreign *Affricamenn* [*Karlamagnus* Saga], or, *blamenn?* If one didn't know any better, based on the difference in nationality and terminology, s/he might argue that today in modern Icelandic *a svertingi* is phenotypically distinct from an *Afrikuma3ur* (svartur). Such quasi differences in terminology are used by the modern scholars to support their argument for a racial difference between the Old Norse *svartr mar,* and native blue skin, i.e., Blaeng, and the foreign *Blalenzkr* or blamadr.

Beyond this point, Hermann Palsson wrote me (in a letter, May 2, 1991) that,

"there is a farm in northern Iceland called Blaland [Africa] (which is now merged with the neighbouring farm of Kjalland), and *it is hard to tell how that name came about. It is certainly very old,* . . . ." (emphasis is mine]. With regard to this African toponym in old Iceland, Palsson suggests: "it is [always] hard to tell how that name came about;" he suggests that it must certainly be "grandiose."

The claims of the modern Old Norse scholars that there were no Africans in medieval Scandinavia appear groundless and unsubstantiated. Even so, the word among them is that the Aryan Model must be maintained. The above article and those like it serve notice to the detractionists that their word at face value no longer suffices. They are not exempt from the burden of proof they demand of everyone else. It is they who are now on the defensive, not serious Afrocentrists. They, like those cited in this article are being called upon to back up their statements with evidence from the primary records, not from later day ideologues. And until they do so, their statements will carry no more weight than the ink used to set them in print.

References

Asante, Molefi. *The Afrocentric Idea.* Philadelphia: Temple University Press, 1987.

_____. "The Ideological Significance of Afrocentricity in Intercultural Communication." *Journal of Black Studies* 14, #1 (September 1983): 3-19.

_____. *Kemet, Afrocentricity and Knowledge.* Trenton: Africa World Press Inc., 1990.

Bernal, Martin. *Black* Athena, vol. 1. New Brunswick: Rutgers University Press, 1987.

Bingham, Caroline. *The Kings and Queens of Scotland.* New York: Dorset Press, 1976.

Bodvarsson, Arni. *Islenzk Ordabok.* Reykjavik: Bokautgafa Menningarsjods, 1963.

Davidson, D. and H. Aldersmith. *The* Great *Pyramid Its Divine Message,* vol. I. London: Williams and Norgate Ltd., 1926.

Derry, T. K. *A History of Scandinavia.* Minneapolis: University of Minnesota Press, 1979.

DeVries, Jan. *Altnordisches Etymologisches Worterbuck.* Leiden: E. J. Brill, 1961.

Diop, Cheikh Anta. *The African Origin of Civilization: Myth or Reality?* Translated by Mercer Cook. Westport: Lawrence Hill, 1974.

_____. *The Cultural Unity of Black Africa.* Paris: Presence Africaine, 1963; reprint, Chicago: Third World Press, 1978.

_____. "The Origin of the Ancient Egyptians." *Unesco General History of Africa* II (1981) 27-57.

Dixon, Roland. *The Racial History of Man.* New York: Charles Scribner's Sons, 1923.

Edwards, Paul. "African Presence in Early Europe," *Research in African Literature,* vol. 18, #3 (Fall 1987): 402-5.

Fell, Christine. *Egils Saga.* London: J. M. Dent and Sons, 1975. Geoffrey of Monmouth. *History of the Kings of Britain.* New York: E. P. Dutton, 1958.

Harvey, John. *The Black Prince and His Age.* London: B. T. Batsford Ltd., 1976.

Holthausen, Ferdinand. *Worterbuch des Altwestnordischen.* Gottingen: Vandenhoeck and Ruprecht, 1948.

James, George G. M. *Stolen Legacy.* New York: Philosophical Library, 1954, reprint, San Francisco: Julian Richardson Associates, 1976.

Johannesson, Alexander. *Islandisches Etymologisches Worterbuch.* Bern: Francke Verlag, 1956.

Jones, Gwyn. *A History of the Vikings.* New York: O~cford University Press, 1968.

Jonsson, Gudni. *Eddulyklar.* Islendingasagnautgafan, 1954.

_____, ed. *Fornaldur Sogur Nordurlanda.* Islendingasagnautgafan, 1954.

Keto, C. Tsehloane. *The African Centered Perspective of History.* Blackwood: K. A. Publications, 1989.

Keyser, R. and C. R. Unger. *Barlaams ok Josaphats Saga.* Christiania: Trykt paa Feilberg & Landmarks Forlag, 1851.

Kristjansson, Jonas, ed. "Viga-Glums Saga," *E Sogur.* Reykjavik: Hid Islenzka Fornritafelag, 1956.

Lauring, Palle. *A History of Denmark.* Kobenhavn: Host and Sons, 1960; reprint translated by David Hohnen. New York: Dorset Press, 1991.

Loyn, H. R. *The Vikings in Bri taro.* London: B. T. Batsford, 1977.

Mackenzie, W. C. The Races *of Ireland and Scotland.* Paisley: Alexander Gardner, n.d.

Magnusson, Asgeir Blondal. *Islensk Ordsifjabok.* Ordabok Haskblans, 1989.

Magnusson, Magnus and Hermann Palsson, trans. *The Vinland Sagas.* Middlesex: Penguin, 1985.

Oakley, Stewart. *A Short History of Denmark.* Washington: Praeger Publishers, 1972.

"Olafs konungs Tryggvasonar." *Fornmanna Sogur* (vols. III, X). Kaupmannahofn: Norraena Fornfraeda Felags, 1827.

 118

Palsson, Hermann and Paul Edwards. *Vikings in Russia.* Edinburgh: The University Press, 1989.

Petersen, N. M., ed. *Egils* Saga. Kebenhavn: Det Nordiske Forlag, 1901.

Rice, Patty C. *Amber: The Golden Gem of the Ages.* New York: Van Nostrand Reinhold Company, 1980.

Rogers, J. A. Nature Knows No Color Line. New York: Helga M. Rogers, 1952.

_____. *100 Amazing facts About the Negro.* New York: Helga M. Rogers, 1970.

_____. *Sex and Race,* vol. I. New York: Helga Rogers, 1967. Saga Sigurdar J~rsalafara." Fornmanna Sogur (vol. VII). Kaupmannahofn: Norraena Fornfraeda-Felags, 1832.

Sayce, A. H. "The Date of Stonehenge," *The Journsal of Egyptian Archeology, I,* pt. 1 (January 1914), 18.

Schach, Paul and Lee M. Hollander, trans. *Eyerbyggja* Saga. Lincoln: University of Nebraska Press, 1959.

Scott, Walter, Sir. *Ivanhoe,* ed. by A. N. Wilson. Middlesex: Penguin, 1984.

Simpson, Jacqueline. *The Viking World.* New York: St. Martin's Press, 1980.

Smith, Elsdon. *American Surnames.* New York: Chilton Book Company, 1969.

Snowden, Frank. *Blacks in Antiquity.* Cambridge: Harvard University Press, 1970.

Sorenson, Sdren. *Ensk-lslenzk Orda bok.* Iceland: Orn og Orlygur, 1984.

Sturluson, Snorri. *Heimskringla.* Translated by Lee M. Hollander. Austin: University of Texas Press, 1964.

Sveinsson, Einar IL., ed. *Laxd~la* Saga. Reykjavik... Islenzk FornritafEelag, 1934.

Svenska Akademien. *Ordbok over Svenska Spraket.* Lund: A. B. PH. Lindstedts Univ. — Bokhandel, 1949.

Welsing, Frances Cress *The Isis Papers.* Chicago: Third World Press, 1991.

Ancient Afrocentric History and the Genetic Model
Clyde A. Winters
Uthman dan Fodio Institute

Cheikh Anta Diop is the precursor to Afrocentricity. Although he never used the term, Diop (1974,1991) laid the foundations for the Afrocentric idea in African historiography. Diop (1974, 1991) has argued that the genetic model can be used to explain the analogy between ancient African civilizations. There are three components in the genetic model: 1) common physical type, 2) common cultural patterns and 3) genetically related languages (Winters, 1989a). Diop over the years has brought to bear all three of these components in his illumination of Kemetic civilization (Diop, 1974,1977,1978,1991).

The foundation of Diop's (1974, 1991) view of ancient African history is that Egypt was a Black Civilization. The opposition of many Eurocentric scholars to Afrocentricity results from White hostility to Diop's idea of a Black Egypt, and the view that Egyptians spoke an African, rather than Afro-Asiatic language. Many Eurocentrists believe that African Americans should only write about slavery and leave the writing of ancient history to more "qualified" scholars. Moitt (1989) observed that: "The limitation has come about of the bias in historiography. The central problem is that historians have made plantation slavery and its effects in the Americas their sole preoccupation. And they have persuaded their students to do likewise. The damage this has done is incalculable. Blacks viewed their history and, by extension that of Africa in terms of slavery" (p. 358).

Moitt (1989) believes that this desire to deny Blacks a role in ancient history is the root cause of White opposition to Diop. He wrote that: "All of this raises the question of historical methodology and goes to the heart of the matter of Diop's isolation....To what must we attribute this negation of Diop? The negation goes beyond the artificial division of the African continent at the Sahara desert and hinges on Diop's ideas the most contentious of which is that the ancient Egyptians were Blacks. In this respect, the negation is not of Diop alone…. Bantu migration, Islam and the slave trade are seen as major problems in African history, the debate over Egypt is stifled" (Moitt, 1989, p. 358).

Recently, Eurocentric American scholars have attempted reviews of Diop's work (Diop 1991). Although these reviewers mention the work of Diop in their articles, they never review his work properly, because they seem to lack the ability to understand the many disciplines that Diop has mastered (Lefkowitz, 1992, 1996; Baines, 1991).

For example Lefkowitz (1992, 1996) summarizes Diop (1974) but never presents any evidence to dispute the findings of Diop. The most popular "review" of Diop (1991) was done by Baines (1991) review in the *New York Times Book Review*. In this "review" Baines (1991) claims that "…the evidence and reasoning used to support the arguments are often unsound". This is the extent of his critique.

Instead of addressing the evidence Diop (1991) presents of the African role in the rise of civilization that he alleges is "unsound", Baines is asking the reader to reject Diop's thesis without refutation of specific evidence presented by Diop of the African contributions to Science and Philosophy. Baines (1991) claims that Diop's *Civilization or Barbarism*, is not a work of originality, he fails to dispute any factual evidence presented by Diop.

Baines (1991) wants the public to accept his general negative comments about *Civilization or Barbarism*, based on the fact that he is an Egyptologist. This is not enough, in academia to refute a thesis one must present counter evidence that proves the falseness of a thesis not unsubstantiated rhetoric. We cannot accept the negative views of Baines on faith alone.

Selected African and African American academics have also attempted to attack Diop (Blakey, 1995; Holl, 1995). Blakey

(1995), like Baines (1991) disputes the findings of Diop but he fails to present any specific criticism of Diop's (1974, 1991) abundant archaeological, linguistic and historical findings denoting an African origin of Egypt. As a result, Blakey (1995) says that Afrocentrists "lack anthropological background" but he does not give one example of this "lack of background" in his long essay attacking Afrocentricity. Indeed, many of the leading Afrocentrists have not only studied anthropology, but other disciplines as well. Holl (1995) an African archaeologist who has made significant discoveries in relation to the ancient empire of Ghana has also recently criticized Diop. Holl (1995) provides a good summary of Diop's methods and research.

Holl (1995) believes incorrectly that Diop's ideas were based on the Pan-Africanist movement and had direct roots in the work of Blyden (1887, 1890, 1905) and Du Bois (1965, 1970). As a result of Diop's participation in the Pan-Africanist movement, Holl (1995, 198, 200) argues that the work of Diop is based on a political agenda.

The main criticism Holl (1995, 207) expresses regarding Diop's work is his identification of Ancient Egypt, Nubia and parts of the Sahara as the original homeland of the people of Senegal. Holl (1995, 207) claims that Diop has failed to support the migration of West Africans from a "Nilotic cradle" in the East, into West Africa. This criticism is unfounded. There is abundant archaeological and linguistic evidence supporting the Saharan origin of the West Africans. Much of West Africa was heavily forested until the last part of the first millennium B.C. (McIntosh & McIntosh, 1983; Winters, 1986). The Niger Delta, for example, was uninhabited until after 500 B.C. (McIntosh & McIntosh, 1983, 39-42). Scholars such as Theophile Obenga and Moussa Lam have demonstrated in their works the linguistic connections of people in Western and Central Africa with the Nile Valley cradle. Indeed, Lam's book on the migration of the Peul from the Nile Valley across the Sahel to present day Senegal is a work of immense methodological significance.

Diop marshaled linguistic and archaeological data to support an Eastern African origin for the people of West Africa. He used toponyms and ethnonyms to prove the migration of West Africans from the Central and eastern Sudan (Diop, 1981). There is other evidence that support an African origin for the West Africans. There are many West African influences in West Africa (Andah, 1981). In addition, the bowl designs from the Niger Delta dating to 250 B.C., are analogous to pottery styles from the southern Sahara to between 2000-500 B.C. (Winters, 1986).

The contemporary archaeological evidence indicates that the Manding people and the Fulani came from the "Nilotic centre" proposed by Diop (Winters, 1986; Ki-Zerbo, 1979). The ancestors of these people belonged to the C-Group culture and formerly lived in the Fezzan and other highland regions of the Sahara (Ki Zerbo, 1979, 32). The inhabitants of the Fezzan were round-headed Africans (Jelinek, 1985, 273). The cultural characteristics of the Fezzanese were analogous to C-Group culture items and the people of Ta-Seti. The C-Group people occupied the Sudan and Fezzan regions between 3700-1300 B.C. (Jelinek, 1985).

The inhabitants of Libya were called Tmhw (Tamehu). The Tamehu were organized into two groups the Thnw (Tehenu) in the North and the Nhsi (Nehasi) in the South (Diop, 1986). A Tehenu personage is depicted on Amratian period pottery (Farid, 1985, 84). The Tehenu wore pointed beards, phallic-sheath and feathers on their head. The Temehu are called the C-Group people by archaeologists (Jelinek, 1985; Quellec, 1985). The central Fezzan was a center of C-Group settlement, these people show culture elements that are analogous to the Fulani and other Senegalese people (Ki Zerbo, 1979; Quellac, 1985). Quellec

(1985, 373) discussed in detail the presence of C-Group culture traits in the Central Fezzan along with their cattle during the middle of the Third millennium B.C..

The Temehu or C-Group people began to settle Kush around 2200 B.C.. The kings of Kush had their capital at Kerma, in Dongola and a sedentary center on Sai Island. The same pottery found at Kerma is also present in Libya especially the Fezzan.

The C-Group founded the Kerma dynasty of Kush. Diop (1986, 72) noted that the "earliest substratum of the Libyan population was a Black population from the south Sahara". Kerma was first inhabited in the 4th millennium B.C. (Bonnet, 1986). By the 2nd millennium B.C. Kushites at Kerma were already worshippers of Amen and they used a distinctive Black-and-red ware (Bonnet, 1986; Winters, 1985b, 1991). Amen, later became a major god of the Egyptians during the 18th Dynasty.

There are similarities between Egyptian and Saharan motifs (Farid, 1985) associated with the ancestors of the Fulanis. It was in the Sahara that we find the first evidence of agriculture, animal domestication and weaving (Farid, 1985, p. 82). This highland region is the Kemites "Mountain of the Moons " region, the area from which the civilization of Kem, originated.

The rock art of the Saharan Highlands, associated with the Fulani, support the Egyptian traditions that in ancient times they lived in the Mountains of the Moon (Winters, 1994). The Pre-dynastic Egyptian mobiliar art and the Saharan rock art share many common themes including, characteristic boats (Farid, 1985, p. 82), men with feathers on their head (Petrie, 1921, pl.xv111, fig. 74; Vandier, 1952, p. 285, fig. 192), false tail hanging from the waist (Vandier, 1952, p. 353; Farid, 1985, p. 83; Winkler, 1938, I, pl.xxlll) and the phallic sheath (Vandier, 1952, p. 353; Winkler, 1938, I, pl.xvlll, xx, xxlll).

Due to the appearance of aridity in the Mountains of the Moon the proto-Saharans migrated first into Nubia and then into Kemet.

 125

The Proto-Saharan origin of the Kemites and the Fulani, explain the fact that the Kushites were known for maintaining the most ancient traditions of the Kemites as proven when the XXVth Dynasty or Kushite Dynasty ruled ancient Egypt. Farid (1985) wrote, "To conclude, it seems that among pre-dynastic foreign relations, the [Proto-] Saharans were the first to have significant contact with the Nile Valley, and even formed a part of the pre-dynastic population" (Farid, p. 85).

The archaeological evidence is clear the Fulani, Mande, and other West African people formerly lived in the Sahara and the Sudan (Ki-Zerbo, 1979; McIntosh and McIntosh, 1983; Winters, 1986). This archaeological evidence confirms the "Nilotic" origin of many West African people as postulated by Diop, and proves that Holl's (1995) criticism of Diop is without merit.

The Black African Origin of Ancient Egyptian Civilization
Language is the sanctum sanctorum of Diop's Afrocentric historical method. The Diopian view of historiography combines the research of linguistics, history and psychology to interpret the cultural unity of African people. Diop has contributed much to African linguistics. He was a major proponent of the Dravidian-African relationship (Diop, 1974, 116), and the African substratum in Indo-European languages in relationship to cacuminal sounds and terms for social organization and culture (1974, 115). Diop (1978, 113) also recognized that in relation to Arabic words, after the suppression of the first consonant, there is often an African root.

Diop's major linguistic effort has been the classification of Black African and Egyptian languages. Until 1977 Diop's major area of interest were morphological and phonological similarities between Egyptian and Black African languages. Diop (1977, 77-84) explains many of his sound laws for the Egyptian-Black African connection. In his book, *Parente Genetique de 1'Egyptien pharaonique et des Langues Negro Africaines* (PGEPLNA), Diop explains in some detail his linguistic views in the introduction of this book. In PGEPLNA Diop demonstrates the genetic relationship between ancient Egyptian and the languages of Black Africa. Diop provides thousands of cognate Wolof and Egyptian terms in support of his Black African-Egyptian linguistic relationship.

Diop (1974) argued that the ancestors of the Kemites (Egyptians) originally lived in Nubia. The Nubian origin of Egyptian civilization is supported by the discovery of artifacts at Qustul by archaeologists from the Oriental Institute at the University of Chicago. On a stone incense burner found at Qustul we find a palace facade, a crowned King sitting on a throne in a boat, with a royal standard placed before the King and hovering above him, the falcon god Horus. The White crown on this Qustul king was later worn by the rulers of Upper Egypt.

Many Egyptologists were shocked to learn in 1979, that the A-Group of Nubia at Qustul used Egyptian type writing two hundred years before the Egyptians (Williams, 1987). This fact had already been recognized much earlier by Diop (1974, 125) when he wrote that it was in Nubia "where we find the animals and plants represented in hieroglyphic writing".

The Qustul site was situated in a country called Ta-Seti. The name Ta-Seti means, "Land of the Bow". Ta-Seti was the name given to Nubia and a southern nome of Kemet. The Qustul incense burner indicates that the unification of Nubia preceded that of Egypt. The Ta-Seti site showed a rich culture at Qustul. Qustul Cemetery L had tombs that equaled or exceeded Kemet tombs of the First Dynasty of Egypt.

The people of Ta-Seti had the same funeral customs, pottery, musical instruments and related artifacts as the Egyptians. Williams (1987, 173, 182) believes that the Qustul Pharaohs are the Egyptian Rulers referred to as the Red Crown rulers in ancient Egyptian documents. Williams (1987) gave six reasons why he believes that the people of Qustul founded Kemet civilization: He identified (1) a direct progression of royal complex designs from Qustul to Hierakonpolis to Abydos, (2) Egyptian objects in Naqada III A and B tombs, (3) No royal tombs in Lower and Upper Egypt, (4) Pharaonic monuments that refer to conflict in Upper Egypt, (5) Inscriptions of the ruler Pe-Hor are older than the inscriptions of Iry-Hor of Abydos, and (6) the ten rulers of Qustul, one at Hierakonpolis and three at Abydos correspond to the historical kings of late Naqada period.

The findings of Williams (1987), support the findings of Diop (1991, p. 108) that "we also understand better now why the Egyptian term designating royalty etymologically means: (the man who comes from the South= nsw< n y swt = who belongs to the South = who is a native of the South = the King of Lower Egypt, and has never meant just King, in other words king of Lower and Upper Egypt, King of all Egypt". The above archaeological evidence makes it clear that theory of the "extreme Eurocentrists" that the Egyptians were White and not Black is groundless. To be king one had to have origins in the South. The king of Lower Egypt was not king.

Four Philosophical Schools

I have identified four philosophical schools associated with an Afrocentric orientation: *perennialist, essentialist, existentialist,* and *progressivist*. I emphasize that these are my terms and have not necessarily been employed by any of the authors to whom I refer. Although the term Afrocentricity gains intellectual currency in the works of Molefi Kete Asante (1980, 1986, 1987, 1990, 1999) that deal with African agency and centeredness, the ideas associated with a positive African response to phenomena might be seen in the works of numerous predecessors. Thus, the taxonomic system I use to classify the various Afrocentric philosophical positions and related values affecting Afrocentricity are modeled on philosophical developments associated with education.

We can use taxonomies of educational philosophies to discuss any proposed Afrocentric curriculum because both education and

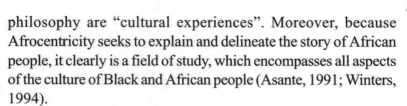

philosophy are "cultural experiences". Moreover, because Afrocentricity seeks to explain and delineate the story of African people, it clearly is a field of study, which encompasses all aspects of the culture of Black and African people (Asante, 1991; Winters, 1994).

The perennialist Afrocentrists studies the classic works of the African tradition. The adherents of this school include Martin Delaney (1978), Edward Blyden (1887, 1905) and Frederick Douglas (1966). These individuals see knowledge as truth, which is eternal. The essentialist Afrocentric school emphasizes in its writing data that are well established through scientific research. Afrocentrists of this philosophical school include W. E. B. Du Bois (1965, 1970), John Jackson (1974), C.A. Winters (1985, 1989, 1991, 1994) and Leo Hansberry (1981). They believe that as new research is published, it should be analyzed for its relevance to the ancient history of African and Black people to enrich our understanding of the past.

The existentialist Afrocentrists believe that Africalogical studies should thrive to teach African people to know more about themselves so we can have a better world. The Afrocentric existentialists include J.A. Rogers, Cheikh Anta Diop (1974, 1991), G.M. James (1954), Marcus Garvey (1966) and A.A. Schomburg (1979).

The final Afrocentric philosophical school is the progressivist. The progressivist Afrocentrist believes that African agency is the principal dimension of a revolutionary philosophy to change the nature of our reality. Thus, the progressivist is always seeking the "centered" place within phenomena to establish how Africans are acting or participating in the creation of the novel. It is a reconstructive approach to culture. The major exponents of this frame of reference are Molefi K. Asante (1991) and Maulana Karenga (1993).

In regards to the Afrocentric view that the Egyptians were Black Africans we must look to the Afrocentric perennialists.

The perennialists founded the Afrocentric ancient history curriculum. The perennialist school is associated with Frederick Douglas (1966) and Martin Delaney (1978). These Afrocentrists writing in the 19th century placed the great works of the past center stage in the formulation of their Afrocentric ancient history knowledge base.

The perennialists postulated that you should use the Bible and the writings of the classical scholars who recognized the "Ancient Model" of history (i.e., Blacks played a major role in ancient history) in deciding on what to teach people about the ancient history of African Americans. The Old Testament provides annals of the ancient Empires of Africa and Mesopotamia.

In the Old Testament the Blacks are recognized as the sons of Ham. According to the Old Testament narrative found in the *Book of Genesis* (10:6), the children of Ham, are alleged to be the founders of all the ancient civilizations including Cush (the Ta Seti, and C-Group cultures of Nubia and the Sudan; the Sumerians of Mesopotamia and the Elamites of Iran), Mizraim (the founder of the Egyptians), Phut (the civilizations of ancient Ethiopia/ South Arabia), and Canaan. The Old Testament narrative and the classical literature was important to the perennialists because it already recognized the division of Black people of Africa into two groups: the Semitic (Canaan and Phut) speakers and Black African (Egypt, Sumer and Elam) speakers (Winters 1985, 1989, 1991).

The archaeological evidence discovered over the past century of Blacks as the founders of the Egyptian, Elamite and Sumerian civilizations validates the perennialists Afrocentric view of ancient history (Diop, 1974; Du Bois, 1965, 1970; Jackson, 1974; Winters, 1985, 1989, 1991, 1994). This body of knowledge discussed in detail by Afrocentric essentialist supports the proposition that we teach students about the immense role of Blacks in the ancient world based on the Classical and Old 17

Testament narratives. This literature provides us with the basis of the "Ancient Model" of world history discussed expertly by Bernal (1987, 1991).

Extreme Eurocentrists like D'Souza (1995) and Lefkowitz (1992, 1996) have assumed that the Afrocentrists are wrong about the prominent role of African/Black people in ancient times. D'Souza (1995) and Lefkowitz (1996) assert that the Afrocentric claims of Africans in ancient America, Asia, Greece and the Egyptian influence over Greece are nothing more than "Afrocentric mythologies of the ancient world" (Lefkowitz, 1996, 157). And, as a result, Lefkowitz claims that the Afrocentrists are not teaching history.

One of the major spokesmen for the Eurocentric view of African history is Dinesh D'Souza. D'Souza, a non-historian, linguist, has made his mission in life the destruction of Multiculturalism, and Afrocentricity in particular, as additions to Afrocentricity fundamentally remains a pedagogy an initiation into a new form of Black consciousness and also into manhood" (p. 360). Given this Eurocentric view of Africalogy, D'Souza sets out to prove that slavery was not racist; that segregation was established by paternal Whites to protect the former slaves; and especially that "Egypt was a multiracial society" dominated by White skinned Egyptians, and that the only time that Blacks / Africans ruled Egypt, was during the Nubian dynasty (p. 367-368). D'Souza (1995, 379) has questioned the Afrocentrists confirmation of the worldwide supremacy of African people before 500 B.C.

The Afrocentric researchers, on the other hand, have long ago proven that Kemet (ancient Egypt) (Diop, 1974; Du Bois, 1965; Winters, 1994), the first two ancient civilizations of China (Xia and Shang) (Winters, 1983d, 1985c), the Pelasgian civilization of Europe (Du Bois, 1965; Parker, 1917, 1918; Winters, 1983b, 1983c, 1984a, 1985, 1994) and civilizations in ancient America (Du Bois, 1965; Rensberger, 1988; van Sertima, 1976;

131

Wiercinski, 1972; Wiener, 1920-1922; Winters, 1977, 1979, 1981/
1982, 1984, 1984b) were founded by Black/African people speaking African languages. Using the ancient model of historical research Bernal (1996), Asante (1996), and Winters (1994) have discussed the classical evidence of an African role in the rise of Greece.

Blacks in Greece

Bernal (1996) on the other hand, argues that some Afrocentrists have "failed" to support some of their claims about the role of African people in ancient history. But overall these Africalogical researchers of the Afrocentric research tradition are presenting a view of history based on the "ancient model" of historical research. Because of the errors in volumes one and two of *Black Athena*, by M. Bernal (1987, 1991) Eurocentrists have attacked the Afrocentrist evidence of an African foundation for Grecian civilization (Lefkowitz, 1992; Pounder 1992; Levine, 1992; Trigger, 1992). Lefkowitz (1992, 1996) has referred to this historical information as "the illusions of Afrocentrists".

Lefkowitz (1992) and Snowden (1992, 1976) perpetuate the myth that the only Blacks in ancient Europe were slaves or mercenaries. This is false; the Greek historical works make it clear that many ancient settlers of the Aegean came from Africa, especially the Garamantes and Pelasgians. Parker (1918) wrote that: "I need not go into details concerning the ethnical relations of the Romans, since they too, are Mediterranean and are closely related to the same African confederation of races as Greece. Aeneas, their mythical founder was in direct descent from Dardanus, the African founder of Troy. The Aenead, like the *Illiad*, and *Odyssey* and all other of the world's great epics, is the poetic story dealing with African people" (Parker, p. 29).

The Eurocentrists attempt to prove there was "considerable cultural and linguistic continuity from the twelfth century to the eighth century B.C." in the Aegean (Lefkowitz, 1992, p.30). Yet there is no way it can be proven that Indo-European Greeks have always been in Greece. This view on the continuity between the Linear B Greeks and later Greeks held by Lefkowitz is disputed by Hopper (1976) who noted that "after all, so much which characterizes Minoan Crete seems wholly alien to later Greece, despite the efforts of scholars to detect 'continuity'" (Hopper, p.xli).

Given the wealth of Afrocentric literature it would seem logical that the "resisters" review these works, and point out the weaknesses within these text to prove that Afrocentricity is a "myth" (Lefkowitz, 1992). But, instead of doing just this, the "resisters" simply mention text written by Afrocentric scholars and then attack *Black Athena*, as if Afrocentricity is based solely on this text.

Black Athena is not the Afrocentric Bible on Black Egypt. We doubt that Cheikh Anta Diop would have even agreed with most of the thesis of this book. Trigger (1992) observed that: Although he [Bernal] has acquired an enthusiastic following among exponents of negritude and occasionally describes some of the Egyptian Pharaohs as "Black" or "Nubian", he aligns himself not with Cheikh Anta Diop but with more moderate "Negro intellectuals...who...do see Egypt as essentially African" (Trigger, p. 121): Bernal (1987, 1991) believes that the Greeks resulted from a mixture of European and (Semitic speaking) Mediterranean people. In volume 2 of *Black Athena* Bernal outlines his thesis that the "Egyptians" founded Greek civilization. But these "Egyptians" are not Blacks, they are Semitic speakers. Bernal (1991) makes it clear that he believes that Semitic speaking Phoenicians, and the Semitic speaking Hyksos Dynasty of Egypt founded the civilization of the Aegean.

Bernal (1991, p. 525) sees the Hyksos invaders as Hurrian, Semitic, Indo-Iranian speakers. As a result he believes that the Danaos and Kadmeans or Egyptian founders of Thebes in Greece, were the Hyksos (Bernal, 1991, p. 495). In general, Bernal (1991)

 133

believes that when the Hyksos were driven from Egypt, they settled in the Aegean and developed civilization. Levine (1992, p. 440) describes *Black Athena*, as "an extraordinarily interesting and dangerous book...dangerous, because in reopening the nineteenth-century discourse on race and origins, the work, sadly, inevitably, has become part of the problem of racism rather than the solution that its author envisioned". Pounder (1992) objects to Bernal (1991) because "Bernal makes a major contribution to confusion and divisiveness by giving credence to Afrocentrist theories that cannot be supported by historical, anthropological, or archaeological criteria" (p. 463).

Bernal's view of the Hyksos as the founders of Grecian civilization has nothing to do with the work of Afrocentric scholars. The problem with Bernal (1991) is that he believes that the "Pre-Hellenes" or Pelasgian people were Indo-European speakers. Afrocentric scholars who recognize that the founders of Athens and Attica were Blacks do not hold this view. (Parker, 1917, 1918; Winters, 1983b) Diop (1974, 1991) and Clyde Ahmad Winters (1983b) make it clear that Blacks came to Greece in prehistoric times. Therefore the apparent errors in Bernal's *Black Athena*, should not be seen as proving that the Afrocentric scholars are wrong. These errors only prove that Bernal (1991) has failed to prove that the Hyksos founded civilization in the Aegean. Afrocentric scholars are accused of using old and outdated sources. This is true of some Afrocentric scholars who have written books based on secondary sources. Yet, those Afrocentric scholars such as Du Bois (1965, 1970), Diop (1974, 1991), J.A. Rogers, Parker (1917, 1918), Winters (1983b, 1985b, 1989a, 1989b) use up-to-date sources to prove their historical facts of the African past.

Even before Diop (1974, 1991) Afrocentric scholars used multiple methods and sources to illuminate the African past. These scholars because of their unique character as a Black people unaware of their specific original African home have not been blinded by ethnocentrism to look for the history of Blacks in one area of

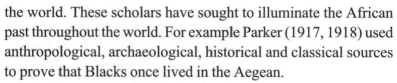

the world. These scholars have sought to illuminate the African past throughout the world. For example Parker (1917, 1918) used anthropological, archaeological, historical and classical sources to prove that Blacks once lived in the Aegean.

Parker (1917, 1918) used the Greek classics to prove that the Pelasgians were of African origin. He also discussed the origin stories about the Pelasgic founders of selected Grecian cities and proved that these men were Blacks and not Indo Europeans (Parker, 1917, 337-338). Parker (1917) also observed that "The great Grecian epics are epics of an African people and Helen, the cause of the Trojan War, must henceforth be conceived as a beautiful brown skin girl" (Parker, pp. 341-42).

In the works of Homer we find that many of the terms have been falsely translated to make it appear that the Greek Heros were a fair skinned race. Parker (1918) noted that:

> ".... let us consider the supposed testimony to the presence of the fair type in Greece and to its superiority over the darker populations....The truth of the matter is that these translators, like historians, have permitted their prejudices to warp their accuracy....Apollo in Homer is *chrysaeros*; that is to say, bearing a golden sword; while *xanthos,* which has been mistranslated to mean fair means brown. Artemis is eustephanos, which has no relation whatever to fair."

Neptune is kyanochaites; that is to say, bluish, Blackish, like the dark deep waves of the ocean. Neither Hera nor Kalypsos are fair from their descriptive adjectives. Achilles is xanthos, which as was said before means brown. Agamemnon is also xanthos, and remember, if you please, that he is in direct descent from Epaphos, the Black ancestor of the Pelasgic house.

Using archaeological evidence and the classical literature Winters (1983b) explained how the African/Black founders of

  135

Grecian civilization originally came from the ancient Sahara. Winters (1983b, pp. 15-16) makes it clear that these Blacks came to the Aegean in two waves 1) the Garamantes a Malinke/Mande speaking people that now live along the Niger River, but formerly lived in the Fezzan region of Libya; and 2) the Egyptians and East Africans who were recorded in Greece's history as the Pelasgians.

The Pelasgian civilization has been discussed in detail by Parker (1917, 1918). The Pelasgians founded many cities. The Pelasgian founding of Athens is noted by Plutarch (1934, 1935). According to Herodotus (para. vii, 91, the Pelasgians also founded Thebes. There is an argument that the Garamantes founded the Greek cities of Thrace, Minoan Crete and Attica (Winters, 1983b). The Garamantes were also called Carians by the Indo-European Greeks. The Garamantes or Carians originally lived in the Fezzan. These Garamantes were described by the classical writers as Black or dark skinned: perusti, *furvi*, and *nigri*. As a result of the research of Parker (1917, 1918) and Winters (1983b), when Lefkowitz (1996, 1992, p. 29) argues that Socrates could not have been Black because he was an Athenian citizen, she fails to prove Socrates' racial heritage because the Greeks made it clear that the founders of Athens were Pelasgians. Lefkowitz (1992, p. 30) notes that if Socrates and his parents had dark skin and other African features, then it is likely that at least some of Socrates's contemporaries would have mentioned it unless all the Athenians had African origins as well. But then why, Lefkowitz asks, does the art not depict the Athenians as Africans? This question is easily answered. There are numerous Africans depicted in Greek art, but rather than admit that some of these Blacks were descendants of the Pelasgian and Garamante groups they are all referred too as Ethiopian slaves or mercenaries (Snowden, 1976).

The work of Diop (1974, 1991), Parker (1917, 1918) and Winters (1983b) establish that the Afrocentric discussion of the

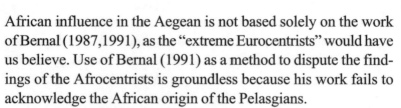

African influence in the Aegean is not based solely on the work of Bernal (1987,1991), as the "extreme Eurocentrists" would have us believe. Use of Bernal (1991) as a method to dispute the findings of the Afrocentrists is groundless because his work fails to acknowledge the African origin of the Pelasgians.

Although Lefkowitz teaches classical studies her research methods leave a lot to be desired. She declares in *Not Out of Africa* that, "there is no archaeological data to support the notion that Egyptians migrated to Greece during the second millennium B.C. (or before that)" (Lefkowitz, 1996, 157).

This view held by Lefkowitz is not exactly correct. In addition to the research of Afrocentrists using classical resources, numerous archaeologists have found abundant evidence of Egyptians settled in Greece long before the coming of the Indo-European-Aryans to Anatolia. Cecil Torr (1896, 61) discussed the inscriptions of Amenhotep found in a Mycenaean tomb at Ialysos in Rhodes and an 18th Dynasty scarab dating to the same period. Torr (1896, 64-65) speculated that there were relations between Egypt and Greece between 1271 and 850 B.C.

The discovery of Torr was only the tip of the iceberg. Archaeological evidence of Egyptians in Greece during the 2nd millennium has also been discussed by J.D.S. Pendlebury (1930), William A. Ward (1971), and S.W. Manning (1995). Pendlebury (1930, xviii-xix) provides a detailed discussion of the Egyptian material found at Laconia, Argolid, Thebes in Boeotia, and Athens. Pendlebury like Torr, believes that there were close relations between Greece and Egypt between the 12th and 7th centuries B.C. (Pendlebury, 1930, 79).

Pendlebury's *Aegyptiaca*, has been excellently followed up by N. J. Skon Jedele (1995), in her recent dissertation on Egyptian artifacts found in Greece. This dissertation provides even more examples of Egyptian artifacts found in Greece than those recorded by Pendlebury over sixty years ago. Manning (1995, 117-118) gives a well-balanced discussion of the Egyptian material found in the Aegean area dating between the Old Kingdom and Dynasties 10 and 11. The work of Hankey and Warren (1989) indicate that there is archaeological evidence for Egyptians in ancient Greece (Warren, 1980), contrary to the false claims of Lefkowitz in *Not Out of Africa*.

The question must be asked, if there is this abundance of literature relating to an Egyptian role in ancient Greece, Why does Lefkowitz fail to discuss this literature? Failure to discuss this relevant knowledge base is inexcusable given Lefkowitz' position in classical studies. The existence of a rich literature on the presence of Egyptians in ancient Greece makes Lefkowitz's claims about the ancient Greeks patently false.

Blacks in Ancient America

Columbus was not the first person from the old world to influence the people and cultures of America. Over 2600 years before Columbus stumbled on the Americas, Africans from West Africa were already establishing the first American civilization in Meso-America (van Sertima, 1976; Wiener, 1920-1922; Winters, 1981/1982).

When the Europeans came to the Americas they discovered Africans were already well established in Latin America Quatrefages, 1889; Rafinesque, 1836; Wiener, 1920-1922; Winters, 1984c, 1984d; Wuthenau, 1980). On Columbus' third voyage he noted Africans sailing in the Caribbean. Other Africans were found in the interior of the Isthmus of Panama. And Bishop Las Casas wrote about an African king residing in the same part of Panama. A. de Quatrefages (1889), claimed that Africans formerly lived in Florida, the Caribbean, Mexico and Panama. The American linguist C.S. Rafinesque (1836) was sure that "many nations of Brazil and Guyana are more recent and of African origin" (p. 9). He also discovered that an Amerind language called Yarura was a Twi cognate. As early as 1700 B.C. the first Africans settled along the Isthmus of Tehuantepe (Winters, 1981,

1982, 1984c). The precursor civilization/empire in the Americas was that of the Olmecs (Morley, 1983; Pouligny, 1988; Soustelle, 1984).

The "extreme Eurocentrists" argue that Blacks could not have been in the Americas in ancient times (D'Souza, 1995; de Montellano, 1995). To support this view these researchers point out that most Americanists do not support an African presence in ancient America, and that van Sertima misidentified the ancestors of the Olmecs (de Montellano, 1995, 139). To explain away the African features of the Olmecs, D'Souza (1995) maintains that:

The Olmecs did not have a selection of skin tones to choose from in making their monuments. The only stone available to them was Black stone. The source of the stone is the Tuxtlas mountains of volcanic origin (p. 374). He continues, "The monuments get darker by thousands of years of exposure to the elements" (D'Souza, 1995, 374).

This explanation by D'Souza (1995) for the large Olmec heads depicting Africans does not hold up under close observation. First of all, the Olmecs used various metals to depict Afro-Olmecs, besides "Black stone", including Jade (von Wuthenau, 1980). This makes the comments of D'Souza false.

A more serious attack on the African origin of the Olmecs has been mounted by de Montellano (1995, 139) who argues that the Olmecs could not have been Nubians or Kushites of the Napata Meroe civilization, as claimed by van Sertima (1976) because the Olmec civilization preceded the civilization of the Kushites by hundreds of years. This argument is well founded. It highlights the failure of van Sertima (1976) to critically read the sources of Africans in ancient America and study the archaeology of West Africa and the Sahara. A cursory reading of Wiener (1922) would have made it clear that the founders of the Olmec civilization were Mande/Manding speaking people.

Wiener (1922) based his identification of the Olmecs (even though he was unaware of this people at the time) through his identification of Manding writing on the Tuxtla statuette, which was created by the Olmecs. Moreover, Wiener (1920-22) provided numerous examples of Manding substratum in Amerindian languages that should have been evaluated by Van Sertima (1976) since he claims to be a linguist. It was the cognition between the Olmec and Manding writings that allowed Winters (1979) to decipher the Olmec writing.

Granted, van Sertima (1976) was wrong about the identity of the Olmecs, but he was correct in claiming that the Olmecs were of African origin. But there is no denying the fact that Africans early settled the Americas (Sitchin, 1990; Wiener, 1920-1922; von Wuthenau, 1980).

The Olmecs were accomplished artists, engineers and scientists. They invented America's first cities, the calendar and writing systems (Soustelle, 1984). This writing system was passed on to the Maya and other people of Mexico (Morley, Brainered & Sharer, 1983; Soustelle, 1984). The Olmecs were the precursor civilization of Meso-America. Jacques Soustelle (1984) called the Olmecs the Sumerians of the New World, due to their great contribution to American civilization. He wrote, "The Olmec heritage was perpetuated in the minds and in the art of the indigenous peoples down to the fall of Tenochlitlan, and still survives in part among the Indians, whose present is profoundly steeped in the past" (Soustelle, 1984, 194).

The Olmec civilization is typified by the huge heads with African features found on many Olmec sites in the Gulf region (van Sertima, 1976; Winters, 1981/1982). The first Olmec head was found at Hueyapan, in the region of San Andres, Tutla, Veracruz (Pouligny, 1988). The name Olmec for this early culture is taken from the term Olman, which was given to the coastal area of the Gulf of Mexico where the artifacts of this culture

 140

were found and Olmeca the name of the inhabitants of this region. The original Or native name for this people was Xi (Shi); the plural form was Xiu (Shi-u).

The Olmec people spoke a Manding language (Winters, 1979; Wuthenau, 1980). The Manding people lived in ancient the Sahara (Winters, 1986), until they migrated to Mexico and founded the Olmec empire (Winters, 1979). The Olmec civilization was developed along the coast of the Gulf of Mexico in the states of Tabasco and Veracruz (Morley, Brainerd & Sharer, 1983, 52; Pouligny, 1988, 34). The linguistic evidence suggests that around 1200 B.C. a new linguistic group arrived on the Gulf region of Mexico. This non-Maya speaking group wedged itself between the Huastecs and the Maya (Swadesh, 1953). Scholars believe that the Olmecs were these new settlers of Mexico (Soustelle, 1984). Soustelle (1984) tells us "We cannot help but think that the people that shattered the unity of the proto-Mayas was also the people that brought Olmec culture." Michael D. Coe (1965:773-774, 1968:121), and Ignacio Bernal (1969:172) support an Olmec origin for the Izapan style art. Quirarte recognized obvious Olmec cultural traits in the Izapa iconography (Quirarte, 1973, 32-33).

The Stelae No.5 from Izapa records many glyphic elements common to other pre-classic artifacts including the jaguar, falling water, mountain, bird, dragon tree, serpent and fish motifs (Smith, 1984, 28-29). The pictures on this stela indicate that the Izapans were related to the Olmec or Xiu people. This stela also provides many elements that relate to Mexican and Maya traditions as accurately analyzed by Norman (1973). Some ideological factors not fully discussed by Norman (1973) in regards to this stela are its evidence of elements of the Olmec religion, and the migration traditions of the Mexicans.

The Maya were not the first to occupy the Yucatan and Gulf regions of Mexico. It is evident from Maya traditions and the

 141

artifacts recovered from many ancient Mexican sites that a different race lived in Mayaland before the Mayan speakers settled this region (Soustelle, 1984). M. Swadesh (1953) has presented evidence that at least 3200 years ago a non- Maya speaking group wedged itself between the Huastecs and the Maya. Soustelle (1984, 29) tells us that the Olmec brought civilization to the region.

Traditions mentioned by Sahagun, record the settlement of Mayaland by a different race from the present Amerindian population. Sahagun (1946) says that these eastern settlers of Mexico landed at Panotha, on the Mexican Gulf. Here they remained for a time until they moved south in search of mountains. Other migrations to Mexico stories are mentioned in the *Popol Vuh*, the ancient religious and historical text compiled by the Quiche Mayan Indians.

Diehl and Coe (1995, 12) of Harvard University have made it clear that until a skeleton of an African is found on an Olmec site he will not accept the art evidence that the were Africans among the Olmecs. This is rather surprising because Constance Irwin and Dr. Wiercinski (1972) have both reported that skeletal remains of Africans have been found in Mexico. Constance Irwin, in *Fair Gods and Stone Faces*, says that anthropologist see "distinct signs of Negroid ancestry in many a New World skull...."

This new race comes from Africa. Van Sertima in *They Came Before Columbus*, and Weiner in *Africa and the Discovery of America* believed that some of these foreign people might have come from West Africa. Wiercinski 1972) claims that some of the Olmecs were of African origin. He supports this claim with skeletal evidence from several Olmec sites where he found skeletons that were analogous to the West African type Black. Wiercinski discovered that 13.5 percent of the skeletons from Tlatilco and 4.5 percent of the skeletons from Cerro de las Mesas were Africoid (Rensberger, 1988).

Many Olmec skulls show cranial deformations (Pailles, 1980). Marquez (1956, 179-80) made it clear that a common trait of the

"Ancient Afrocentric History and the Genetic Model"
Clyde A. Winters
Uthman dan Fodio Institute

African skulls found in Mexico include marked prognathousness, prominent cheekbones are also mentioned. Fronto-occipital deformation among the Olmec is not surprising because cranial deformations was common among the Mande speaking people until fairly recently (Desplanges, 1906).

Friar Diego de Landa, in *Yucatan Before and After the Conquest*, wrote, "Some old men of Yucatan say that they have heard from their ancestors that this country was peopled by a certain race who came from the East, whom God delivered by opening for them twelve roads through the sea" (de Landa, 1978, 8, 28). This tradition is most interesting because it probably refers to the twelve migrations of the Olmec people. This view is supported by the stone reliefs from Izapa, Chiapas, Mexico published by the New World Foundation (see figure 1). In Stelae No.5, from Izapa we see a group of men on a boat riding the waves and a large tree in the middle of the Stelae No.5 (Norman, 1976).

It is clear that Stelae No.5, from Izapa not only indicates the tree of life, it also confirms the tradition recorded by Friar Diego de Landa (1978) that the Olmec people made twelve migrations to the New World. This stela also confirms the tradition recorded by the famous Mayan historian Ixtlixochitl, that the Olmec came to Mexico in "ships of barks" and landed at Pontochan, which they commenced to populate.

In the center of the boat on Stelae No.5, we find a large tree. This tree has seven branches and twelve roots. The seven branches probably represent the seven major clans of the Olmec people. The twelve roots of the tree extending into the water from the boat probably signifies the "twelve roads through the sea", mentioned by Friar Diego de Landa (1978, 8, 28). The migration traditions and Stelae No.5, probably relates to a segment of the Olmec, who landed in boats in Panotha or Panotla (the Huasteca) and moved along the coast as far as Guatemala. This landing in Panotla would correspond to the non-Maya speaking group

143

detected by Swadesh (1953) that separated the Maya and Huasteca speakers over 2000 years ago. Bernardino de Sahagun (1946) a famous authority on Mexico also supports the extra-American origin of the Olmecs when he wrote "Eastern settlers of Mexico landed at Panotla on the Mexican Gulf. Here they remained for a time until they moved south in search of mountains".

Sahagun (1946) claimed that the Olmec were not native to the Gulf coats region where archaeologist discovered the Olmec civilization. He called these people that civilized the Mexicans: Olmecs. Chimalpahin, the chronicler of Chalco Amaquemecan, commenting on the Olmecs said "...the truth is that those who for the first time came to settle, who made merits for the land were great men, very experienced, they were learned men, they were skilled at everything. And because they were skilled learned men, everything they did they always affirmed it" (Portilla, n.d., 193).

Traditions mentioned by Sahagun, record the settlement of Mexico by a different race from the present Amerindian population, these foreign people he called Olmecs. Sahagun said:

> "Here is the account that the elders used to pronounce: at a time which no one can speak of any more, that today no one can remember, those who came here to sow the grandfathers, the grandmothers, these, it is said, arrived, came, followed the road, those that came to sweep it...came to rule here in this land.... They came in many groups in their boats. They arrived at the edge of the water, on the northern coast, and there where their boats remained is called Panutla, which means where one passes over the water, today it is called Pantla (Panuco). Subsequently they followed the shoreline, they went in search of the mountains...."
> (Portilla, n.d., 184-185). Not only did these ancient settlers of the Olmec heartland settle in Mexico, they also helped spread civilization.

 144

Sahagun wrote:

"So they [Olmecs] invented the reckoning of the destinies, the annals, and the reckoning of the years, the book of dreams, they put it in the order in which it has been kept..." (Portilla, n.d., 186). These passages from Sahagun makes it clear that the Olmec people came to Mexico by sea in boats. It would appear that there was not a single settlement of migrants from across the sea because Sahagun claims, "they came in many groups". This may be a possible allusion to the twelve migrations mentioned by de Landa (1978), and recorded on Stelae No.5. It also agrees with the migration story mentioned in the *Popol Vuh*.

The Stelae Number 5 And Olmec Religion

The Olmec people had their own writing. This writing system was deciphered by Winters (Winters, 1979, 80; Wuthenau, 1980, Appendix B). This decipherment of the Olmec writing allows us to discover much about the Olmec people and their culture. We know that the Olmec invited the writing system, which was later used by the Maya because the Mayan name for writing is of Manding/Olmec writing. Kaufman (1976) has suggested that *c'ib' or *c'ihb' is part of the proto-Mayan lexicon *C'ib' may be the ancient Mayan term for writing, but it can not be Proto-Mayan because writing did not appear among the Maya until 600 B.C. This was 1500 years before the break up of Proto-Mayan. The Manding term for writing is *sebe. This term corresponds to the Mayan term *c'ib' and probably was the ancestral name for writing in ancient America introduced by the Olmec people.

There is a Mayan tradition that they got writing from the "Tutul Xiu" who lived in Zuiva. As mentioned earlier the name Xiu is the name of the Manding speaking people. The two Olmec religious associations (ga-fa): the jaguar-man or humano-feline cult and the humano-bird cult. The humano-feline cult was called

145

the names-tigi by the Olmecs, while the humano-feline cult was called the kuno-tigi.

The leader of the Olmec cult was called the tigi or amatigi "head of the faith". The Tigi of the Xiu or Olmec secret societies and cults exerted considerable influence over both the when he was dead and alive. Alive the Tigi could contact the spirits of the deceased, and serve as intermediary between the gods and mankind. Upon his death his grave became a talisman bestowing good to all who visited his tomb.

Van Sertima (1976) and Wiener (Wiener, 1920-1922) have both commented on the possible relationship between the Amanteca of ancient Mexico and the Amantigi of Africa and the Olmecs. It is interesting to note that according to Wiener tec / tecqui means "master, chief" in a number of Mexican languages including Nahuatl. Many Meso-Americanists have suggested that the Maya inherited many aspects of their civilization, especially religion from the Olmec. This is interesting because in the Maya *Book of the Chumayel*, the three main cult associations, which are supposed to have existed in ancient times, were (1) the stone (cutters) cult, (2) the jaguar cult and (3) the bird cult. In lines 4-6 of the *Book of the Chumayel*, we read: "Those with their sign in the bird, those with their sign in the stone, flat worked stone, those with their sign in the Jaguar-three emblems".

The *Book of the Chumayel* corresponds to the glyphs depicted on Monument 13 at La Venta (Bernal, 1969). On Monument 13, at La Venta a personages in profile, has a headdress on his head and wears a breechcloth, jewels and sandals, along with four glyphs listed one above the other. The glyphs included the stone, the jaguar, and the bird emblems. Monument 13, at La Venta also has a fourth sign to the left of the personage, a foot glyph. This monument has been described as an altar or a low column (Bernal, 1969). The foot in Olmec is called se, this symbol means to "lead or advance toward knowledge, or success".

The se (foot) sign of the komow (cults) represents the beginning of the Olmec initiates pursuit of knowledge.

The meaning of Monument 13, reading from top to bottom, is a circle kulu/ kaba (the stone), nama (jaguar) and the keno (bird). The interpretation of this column reading from left to right is "The advance toward success—power—for the initiate is obedience to the stone cutters cult, jaguar cult and the bird cult".

The Jaguar mask association dominated the Olmec Gulf region. In the central and southern Olmec regions we find the bird mask association (cult) predominate as typified by the Xoc bas relief of Chiapas, and the Bas Relief No.2, of Chalcatzingo. Another bird mask cult association was located in the state of Guerrero as evidenced by the humano-bird figure of the Stelae from San Miguel Amuco.

The iconographic representation of the Olmec priest-kings, found at Chalchapa, La Venta, Xoc and Chalcatzingo indicate that usually the Olmec priest wore a wide belt and girdle. He was usually clean-shaven, with an elongated bold head often topped by a round helmet or elaborate composite mask. During religious ceremonies the Olmec religious leader, depending on his cult would wear the sacred jaguar or sacred bird mask. Often as illustrated by the glyphs on the shoulders and knees of the babe in-arms figurine of Las Limas element the mask would include a combination of the associated with the bird, jaguar and serpent.

The cult leaders of the bird mask cult usually wore claws on their feet. The jaguar cult leaders usually wore the jaguar mask. Stelae No.5 also discusses in detail the two major Olmec religions: the nama (jaguar) komo (cult) and the keno (bird) cult. At the top of Stelae No.5, we recognize two lines of Olmec writing across the top of the artifact. ~ U/ On the first line we read from right to left :I ba i. Lu to lu. I ba i, which means, "Thou art powerful Now! Hold Upright (those) obedient to the[ir] Order. Thou art Powerful Now!" On the second line we read the following I lu

147

be. I lu, which means, "Thou hold upright Unity. Thou [it] upright".

The religious orders spoken of in this stela are the Bird and Jaguar cults. These Olmec cults were Nama or the Humano Jaguar cult; and Kuno or Bird cult. The leader of the Mama cult was called the Nama-tigi (Nama chief), or Amatigi (head of the faith). The leader of the Keno cult was the Keno-tigi (Keno chief). These cult leaders initiated the Olmec into the mysteries of the cult.

On the Stelae No.5, we see both the Ruao-tigi (fig.2) and Nama-tigi (fig.3) instructing youth in the mysteries of their' respective cults. On Stelae No. 5, we see two priests and members of each cult society sitting in a boat with a tree in the center (Sitchin, 1990, 178). On the right hand side of the boat we see the Nama tigi, and on the left hand side we see the Kuno-tigi.

The personage on the right side of the boat under a ceremonial umbrella is the Nama-tigi. In Mexico, this umbrella was a symbol of princely status. Above his head is a jaguar glyph which, according to Alexander von Wuthenau (1980) indicates that he was an Olmec. This personage has an African style hairdo and a writing stylus in his left hand. This indicates the knowledge of writing among the Olmecs which is also evident in the other Olmec inscriptions deciphered by Winters. On the sides of the boat we see two Olmec signs Po, ~7 be= Pab~ they read: "In the company of Purity". This statement signifies that the Olmec believed that worship of the Keno or Nama cults led to spiritual purity among the believers.

On the left hand side of the boat we see a number of birds. Here we also find a priest wearing a conical hat instructing another youth, in the mysteries of the Kuno cult around a flame. Among the Olmecs this flame signified the luminous character of knowledge. The Kuno priest wears a conical hat. The evidence of the conical hat on the Kuno priest is important evidence of the Manding in ancient America. The conical hat in Meso-America

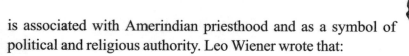

is associated with Amerindian priesthood and as a symbol of political and religious authority. Leo Wiener wrote that:

"That the kingly and priestly cap of the Magi should have been preserved in America in the identical form, with the identical decoration, and should, besides, have kept the name current for it among the Mandingo [Malinke-Bambara/Manding] people makes it impossible to admit any other solution than the one that the Mandingoes established the royal offices in Mexico" (author's emphasis) (Wiener, Vol.2 1922, 321).

Stelae No.21 , from Izapa also record the decline of the Olmec nama and kuno religions and probable raise of the Maya speakers and the sa (serpent) cult which called for human sacrifice (Smith, 1984; Norman, 1973). On Stelae No.21, we see a decapitated individual lying on the ground. An elite carries the decapitated head. This elite may be an early Maya personage because he wears a new style headdress which resembles the Maya style headdresses and not the style of the Olmecs.

In the background we see an elite personage being borne in an elaborate sedan chair. Above this chair we see the serpent. This depiction of a serpent as a background but dominant figure in Olmec religion/rule corresponds to Monument 19 of La Venta. On Monument 19, from La Venta we see an Olmec personage, which has a serpent behind his back and above his head (Bernal, 1969). This serpent indicates hidden knowledge or powers from the serpent that the cult leader used to lead the followers of their cult.

The Olmecs constructed complex pyramids and large sculptured monuments weighing tons. The Maya during the Pre-Classic period built pyramids over the Olmec pyramids to disguise the Olmec origin of these pyramids. After 100 B.C. the Olmecs went into a period of decline. They did not disappear from Mexican history. They were frequently depicted in Mayan text as gods and merchants, especially the Maya god Ek Chuah (Winters, 1981,

 149

1982, 1984a, 1984b, 1984C). The African god Quetzacoatl was worshipped by the Aztecs (Wiener, 1922; Winters, 1981/1982).

African Influence on Amerindian Languages

The Mande/Manding speaking Olmecs had a great influence on the cultural and linguistic realities of the Americas. As a result we find that many Amerindian languages show affinity to the Manding languages. The Taino and Manding languages share many points of phonology and morphology. Taino was spoken in the Caribbean when Europeans first arrived in the New World. Taino is presently extinct. Taino and Manding are agglutinative languages. The joining of two or more words is commonly used to form new words. For example, Manding words are formed by adding an affix to a radical e.g., ji 'water': ji-ma 'watery and ba 'finish': to-ba 'to complete'/'to achieve'. In Taino, we have a 'water': a-ma 'great water'; and ca 'soil': ca-za-bi 'bread'. The Taino and Manding languages share lexical items from the basic vocabulary e.g., mother Manding (M.) bi, Taino (T.) ba; dwelling: M. bo, T. ba; ocean: M. ba, T. ball; son: M. le, T. e3; and god: M. jo (/gyo), T. io. Taino and Manding have similar syntax e.g., Taino teitoca 'you be quiet'; and Manding i-te-to ka 'you be at ease'.

The Otomi people of Mexico are often believed to have been of African origin (Quatrefages, 1889). This is proven by a comparison of the Manding and Olmec languages. The Mezquital Otomi pronominal system shows some analogy to that of Manding, but Neve y Molina's Otomi pronouns show full agreement e.g., Otomi ma/i,e,/a, and Manding n',m' /i,e /a. They also share many cognates from the basic vocabulary including son/daughter: Otomi (O.) t?i or ti, Manding (M.) de/di; eyes: O. da, M. do ; brother: ku, M. koro ; sister: O. nkhu, M. ben-k ; lip: O. sine, M. sine; mouth O. ne, M. ne; and man: O. to/ye, M. tye/kye.

The Otomi and Manding languages also have similar syntax, e.g., Otomi ho ka ra 'ngu 'he makes the houses', Manding a k nu 'he makes the family habitation (houses)'. There are many Maya and Manding cognates, e.g., Maya (My.) naa.l 'parent, mother', Manding (M.) na id.; father: My. ba, M. pa; lord: My. ba, M. ba; maize: My. kan, M. ka. It is interesting to note that in the Amerind languages are characterized by first person /nj, and second person /m/. But in the case of the Otomi and Maya languages we find first person /n/, second a/i , third person /a/, the same pronoun pattern found in the Manding group.

Africans in Early Asia

In addition to recognizing the African influence in Egypt (Diop, 1974, 1991; Winters, 1994) when teaching an Afrocentric ancient history we must also acknowledge that Blacks lived in ancient Asia (Winters, 1983d, 1985a, 1985b, 1989a, 1990, 1991, 1994b). Diop (1974) claimed that Blacks were settled in West Asia in ancient times. Diop (1977,p.xxi) mentions the Black presence in Asia. He also outlined the rise of the Semitic race as a result of the mixing of Blacks in North Africa and West Asia, with the Indo European speaking Sea Peoples after 1300 B.C. (Diop, 1977, pp. xxix-xxx). Diop (1974) also made it clear that the archaeological evidence from Iraq and Iran suggested that the Elamites and Sumerians were Blacks.

Winters (1985b, 1991,1994) has discussed the common Proto Saharan origin for the Sumerians, Egyptians, Dravidians and other African peoples. He has also discussed the fact that these people possessed a common writing system (Winters, 1985a) and language (Winters, 1989a, 1994b). Blacks also founded civilization in China (Winters, 1983d, 1985c, 1988, 1989b, 1990). They founded both the Xia and Shang civilizations (Winters, 1983d, 1986b). The Xia dynasty was the first civilization in China.

The Shang people came from Africa and founded civilization along China's rivers (Winters, 1983d, 1986b). The first King of China was called xuan wang 'Dark Ring'. The founder of Shang

 151

was called xuan niao "Black Bird", another Shang King was called xuan mu " Black Oxen" (1985c). The Shang people were recognized as Blacks by the Chinese (Winters, 1985c; Lacouperie, 1891). They called the Shang rulers xuan di " Black Emperor". The African masses in China were called li min "Black heads" by the Chinese. The Shang and Xia are recognized by art historians for their work in bronze (1985c, 1986b). Shang artists made fine pottery and bronze vases of different shapes, often standing on three legs. In general the Shang had a highly developed technology.

In conclusion, using the genetic model developed by Diop (1991) we discover that Black African people played a prominent role in the raise and development of ancient civilizations. We also learned that as a result of the Afrocentric paradigms developed by Africalogical researchers, such as Maulana Karenga, Ama Mazama, Ruth Reviere, and Molefi Kete Asante, we have been able to fully document the early history of Black/ African people.

Granted, some of the critics of Afrocentric ancient history have made some valid points about the use of dated sources about many of research projects, but overall much of their criticism is invalid. For example, there is an abundance of evidence that indicates that the Egyptians and other Blacks, known to the Greeks as Pelasgians were settled in the Aegean area long before Indo-European speaking nomads arrived on the scene. Moreover, the evidence of African skeletons and writing in the Americas make it obvious that the Olmec people were Africans who spoke an aspect of the Manding language. It is also clear that Stelae No.5, from Izapa not only indicates the tree of life, it also confirms the tradition recorded by Friar Diego de Landa that the Olmec people made twelve migrations to the New World. This stela also confirms the tradition recorded by the famous Mayan historian Ixtlixochitl, that the Olmec came to Mexico in "ships of barks " and landed at Pontochan, which they commenced to populate (Winters, 1984: 16).

 152

"Ancient Afrocentric History and the Genetic Model"
Clyde A. Winters
Uthman dan Fodio Institute

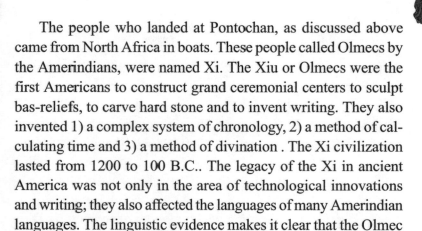

The people who landed at Pontochan, as discussed above came from North Africa in boats. These people called Olmecs by the Amerindians, were named Xi. The Xiu or Olmecs were the first Americans to construct grand ceremonial centers to sculpt bas-reliefs, to carve hard stone and to invent writing. They also invented 1) a complex system of chronology, 2) a method of calculating time and 3) a method of divination . The Xi civilization lasted from 1200 to 100 B.C.. The legacy of the Xi in ancient America was not only in the area of technological innovations and writing; they also affected the languages of many Amerindian languages. The linguistic evidence makes it clear that the Olmec language is a substratum language of Taino and the Mayan languages.

Finally, the evidence is clear Blacks founded many ancient civilizations. The work of Anselin (1982, 1984,1989), Diop (1974, 1991), Du Bois, Winters (1983a, 1983c, 1985a, 1991, 1994, 1994b) and J.A. Rogers all support the influence of Blacks in ancient history and make it a field of study based on a rigorous tradition of scholarship. This should encourage all teachers to teach their students about the great ancient heritage of Blacks.

References

Adler, J. (1991 September 23). "African Dreams", Newsweek. pp. 42-45.

Andah, B. *Wai. West Africa Before the Seventh Century.* In G. Mokhtar (Ed.), General History of Africa, Vol. 2 (pp. 593-619). Berkeley: Heinemann.

Anselin, A. (1982). *Le mythe d' Europe.* Paris: Editions Anthropos.

_____. (1989). "Le Lecon Dravidienne", Carbet Revue Martinique de Sciences Humaines, no.9: 7-58.

Asante, M.K. (1990) *Kemet, Afrocentricity and Knowledge.* Trenton, NJ: Africa World Press.

_____. (1991). "The Afrocentric Idea in Education", Journal of Negro Education, 60(2): 170-180.

_____. (December 1991/January 1992). "Afrocentric Curriculum" Educational Leadership, pp. 28 -31.

Baines, J. (11 August, 1991). "Was Civilization Made in Africa?" The New York Times Review of Books, pp. 12-13.

Bernal, M. (1969). *The Olmec World.* Los Angeles: University of California Press.

Bernal, M. (1996, Spring). *The Afrocentric interpretation of history: Bernal replies to Lefkowitz,* Journal of Blacks in Higher Education, 86-95.

Bernal, M. (1987). *Black Athena*. New York: Free Association Press. Volume 1.

_____. (1991). *Black Athena*. New York: Free Association Press. Volume 2.

Blakey, M.L. (1995). *Race, Nationalism, and the Afrocentric Past*. In P.R. Schmidt and Thomas C. Patterson (Eds.) Making Alternative Histories, Santa Fe, NM: School of American Research Press, pp. 213-228.

Blyden, E.W. (1887). *Christianity, Islam and the Negro Race*. a Edinburgh: Edinburgh University Press.

_____. (1890). *The African Problem and the Method for its Solution*. Washington, D.C.: Gibson Brothers.

Coe, M.D. (1965). *The Olmec Style and its Distribution*. Austin: University of Texas, pp. 739-75.

_____. (1968). *America's First Civilization*. New York: American Heritage.

Davies, A.M. (1986). *The linguistic evidence, is there any?* In G. Cadogan (Ed.), The End of the early Bronze Age in the Aegean (pp. 93-123). London: E. J. Brill.

Delany, M.R. (1978). *The Origin of Races and Color*. Baltimore, M.D.: Black Classic Press.

D'Souza, D. (1995). *The End of Racism*. New York: The Free Press.

Diehl, R.A., & Coe, M.D. (1995). "Olmec Archaeology". In Jill Guthrie (Ed.), Ritual and Rulership, (pp. 11-25). The Art Museum: Princeton University Press.

Diop, C.A. (1974). *The African Origin of Civilization*. (Trans.) Mercer Cook, Westport: Lawrence Hill & Company.

_____. (1977). *Parente Genetique de l'Egyptian pharaonique et des Langues Negro-Africaines*. Dakar: IFAN , Les Nouvelles Editions Africaines.

_____. (1978). *The Cultural Unity of Black Africa*. Chicago: Third World Press.

_____. (1981). *A Methodology for the Study of Migration*. In African Ethnonyms and Toponyms. (ed.) by UNESCO, (Paris: UNESCO), pp. 87-110.

_____ 1986). "Formation of the Berber Branch". In Libya and Antigua. (ed.) UNESCO, (Paris: UNESCO) pp. 69-73.

_____. (1987). *Precolonial Black Africa* (trans.) Harold Salemson, Westport: Lawrence Hill~& Company.

_____. (1988). *Nouvelles les recherches sur l'Egyptien ancient et les langues Negro-Africaines Modernes*. Paris: Presence Africaine.

_____. (1991). *Civilization or Barbarism: An Authentic Anthropology*. (trans.) by Yaa-Lengi Meema Ngemi and (ed.) by H.J. Salemson and M. de Jager, Westport: Lawrence Hill and Company.

Du Bois, W.E.B. (1970). *The Negro*. New York: Oxford University Press.

Du Bois, W.E.B. (1965). *The World and Africa*. New York International Publishers Co., Inc.

Garvey, M. (1966). *Who and What is a Negro?* In H. Brotz (Ed.) Negro social and Political Thought (pp. 560-562). New York: Basic Books.

Graves, Robert. (1980). *The Greek Myths*. Middlesex: Penguin Books Ltd. 2 volumes.

Holl, A.F.C. (1995). *African History: Past, Present and Future*. P.R. Schmidt and Thomas C. Patterson (Eds.), Making Alternative Histories (pp. 183-212), Santa Fe, NM: School of American Research Press.

Hopper, R.J. (1976). *The Early Greeks*. New York: Harper & Row Publishers Hochfield, S. and Riefstahl, E. (1978). (Eds.) Africa in Antiquity: The Arts of Nubia and the Sudan. New York: Brooklyn Museum. 2 vols.

Hansberry, L.H. (1981). *Africa and Africans: As Seen by Classical Writers (Vol. 2)*. Washington, D.C.: Howard University Press.

Jackson, J. (1974). *Introduction to African Civilization*. Secaucus, N.J.: Citadel Press.

James, G.M. (1954). *Stolen Legacy*. New York: Philosophical Library.

Ki-Zerbo, Joseph. (August-September, 1979). *Old Masters of the New Stone Age*. The UNESCO Courier, 27-34.

Lacouperie, Rerrien de. (1891). *The Black Heads of Babylonia and Ancient China*, The Babylonian and Oriental Record, (11), 233-246.

Landa, Friar Diego de, (1978). Y*ucatan Before and After the Conquest* (trans) by William Gates, New York: Dover Pub. Inc.

Levine, M.M. (April 1992). "The Use and Abuse of Black Athena", American Historical Review, pp. 440-460.

Lefkowitz, M. (1992, February 10). *Not Out of Africa*. The New Republic, pp. 29-36.

McIntosh, S.K. and McIntosh, R. (1983). *Forgotten Tells of Mali*, Expedition, 35-47.

Morley, S.G., Brainered, G.W. and Sharer, R.J. (1983). *The Ancient Mayan*, Stanford: Stanford University Press.

Pouligny, D. (1988). *Les Olmeques Archeologie*, 12, 30-36.

Rensberger, B. (September, 1988). "Black Kings of Ancient America", Science Digest, 74-77 and 122.

Manning, S.W. (1995). *The Absolute Chronology of the Aegean Early Bronze Age*. Sheffield: Sheffield Academic Press.

Marriott, M. (1991, August 11). "As a Discipline Advances, Questions Arise on Scholarship". The New York Times.

Martel, E. (December 1991/January 1992). "How Valid are the Portland Baseline Essays". Portland, Oregon. pp. 20-23.

_____. (1991). "Teachers' Corner: Ancient Africa and the Portland Curriculum Resource", Anthropology Notes: National Museum of Natural History, Smithsonian Bulletin for Teachers 13, pp. 2-6.

Moitt, B. (1989). "Cheikh Anta Diop and the African Diaspora: Historical Continuity and Socio-Cultural Symbolism", Presence Africaine. no. 149-150: 347-360.

Montellano, Bernard Ortiz de. (1995). *Multiculturalism, Cultural Archaeology, and Pseudo-science*. In Francis B. Harrold and Raymond A. Eve (Eds.), Cult Archaeology & Creationism (pp. 134-151). Iowa City: University of Iowa Press.

Morley, S.G., Brainerd, G.W., Sharer, R.J. (1983). *The Ancient Mayans*. Stanford, C.A.: Stanford University Press.

Okafor, V.O. (1991). "Diop and the African Origin of Civilization: An Afrocentric Analysis". Journal of Black Studies 22 (2): 252-268.

Norman, V.G. (1976). *Izana Sculpture*. New World Archaeological Foundation, No. 30. University of Utah Press.

Parker, G.W. (1917). "The African Origin of Grecian Civilization" Journal of Negro History, 2(3): 334-344.

_____. (1981). *The Children of the Sun*. Baltimore, Md.: Black Classic Press.

Pendlebury, J.D.S. (1930). *Aegyptica: A Catalogue of Egyptian Objects in the Aegean Area*, Cambridge: Cambridge University Press.

Petrie, W.M.F. (1921). *Corpus of Prehistoric Pottery*. London.

Leon-Portilla, M. (n.d.) "Chimalpahin's use of a testimony by Sahagun: The Olmecs in Chalco-Amaquemecan". In J. Jorge Klor de Alva, H.B. Nicholson and Eloise Quinones Keber (Eds.), The Work of Bernardino de Sahagun (1937). Albany N.Y.: The University of Albany.

Pounder, R.L. (1992, April). "Black Athena 2: History without Rules" American Historical Review, 461-464.

Ravitch, D. (1990, Summer). "Multiculturalism: E Pluribus Plures". The American Scholar, pp. 337-354.

Sahagun, B. de (1946). *Historia General de las Casas de la Nueva Espana*, Mexico City: Editoria Nueva Espana .

Schomburg, A.A. (1979). *Racial Integrity*. Baltimore, M.D.: Black Classic Press.

Sitchin, Z. (1990). *The Lost Realms*. New York: Avon Books.

Smith, V.G. (1984). *Izapa Relief Carving*. Studies in Pre Columbian Art and Archaeology, No.27. Washington, D.C. Dumbarton Oaks.

Soustelle, J. (1984). *The Olmecs: The Oldest Civilization in Mexico*. Garden City, N.Y.: Doubleday.

Skon-Jedele, N.J. (1995). *Aigyptica: A Catalogue of Egyptian and Egyptianized Objects Excavated from Greek Archaeological Sites*. Unpublished Doctoral Dissertation, University of Pennsylvania, Philadelphia.

Swash, M. (1953). The Language of the Archaeological Huastecs. Carnegie Institutions Notes on Middle American Archaeology and Ethnology. no.114. Washington, D.C.

Snowden, F. (1976). "Ethiopians and the Greco-Roman World". In The African Diaspora. Washington: Howard University Press.

_____. (1992, March 4). "Blacks as Seen by Ancient Egyptians, Greek and Roman Artists". (Lecture) Chicago: Oriental Institute of the University of Chicago.

Torr, C. (1896). *Memphis and Mycenae*, London: Cambridge University Press.

Trigger, B.G. (1987). "Egypt: A Fledging Nation". The Journal of the Society for the Study Egyptian Antiquities. 17 (1/2): 58-65.

_____. (1992). "Brown Athena: A Post Processual Goddess". Current Anthropology. 33(1): 121-123.

Vandier, J. (1952). *Manuel d'archeologie Egyptienne*. Paris: Picard.

von Wuthenau, Alexander. (1980). *Unexplained Faces in Ancient America*, 2nd Edition, Mexico 1980.

Ward, W. (1971). *Egypt and the Mediterranean World 2200-1900 B.C.*, Beirut: American University of Beirut.

Warren, P.M. (1980). Problems of Chronology in Crete and the Aegean in the Third and Second Millennium B.C.", American Journal of Archaeology, 84, 487-499.

Warren, P.M. and Hankey, V. (1989). Aegean Bronze Age Chronology, Bristol: Bristol Classical Press.

Wiercinski, A. (1972). *Inter-and Intrapopulational Racial Differentiation of Tlatilco, Cerro de Las Mesas, Teotihuacan, Monte Alban and Yucatan Maya*, XXX1X Congreso Intern. de Americanistas, Lima 1970 , Vol. l, 231-252.

Wiercinski, A. and Jairazbhoy, R.A. (1975). "Comment", The New Diffusionist, 5 (18),5.

Williams, B. (1987). *The A-Group Royal Cemetery at Qustul: Cemetery L*. Chicago: The Oriental Institute University of Chicago.

Winkler, H.A. (1938). *Rock Drawings of Southern Upper Egypt*. London: Egypt Exploration Society. 2 volumes.

Winters, C.A. (1977). "The Influence of the Mande Scripts on Ancient American Writing Systems", Bulletin de l' IFAN, T39, serie B, no. 2 (1977), pp. 941-967.

Winters, C.A. (1979). "Manding Scripts in the New World", Journal of African Civilizations, 1(1), 80-97.

Winters, C.A. (December 1981/ January 1982). *Mexico's Black Heritage*. The Black Collegian, 76-84.

Winters, C.A. (1983a). "The Ancient Manding Script". In Blacks in Science: Ancient and Modern. (ed.) by Ivan van Sertima, (New Brunswick: Transaction Books) pp. 208-215.

_____. (1983b). "Les Fondateurs de la Grece venaient d'Afrique en passant par la Crete". Afrique Histoire (Dakar), no. 8: 13-18.

_____. (1983c). "Famous Black Greeks Important in the Development of Greek Culture". Return to the Source, 2(1): 8.

_____. (1983d). "Blacks in Ancient China, Part 1, The Founders of Xia and Shang", Journal of Black Studies (2), 8-13.

_____. (1984a). "Blacks in Europe Before the Europeans". Return to the Source, 3(1): 26-33.

Winters, C.A. (1984b). *Blacks in Ancient America*, Colorlines, 3 (2), 27-28.

Winters, C.A. (1984c). Africans Found First American Civilization, African Monitor, 1, pp. 16-18.

_____. (1985a). "The Indus Valley Writing and related Scripts of the 3rd Millennium B.C.". India Past and Present. 2(1): 13-19.

_____. (1985b). "The Proto-Culture of the Dravidians, Manding and Sumerians". Tamil Civilization.3 (1): 1-9.

_____. (1985c). "The Far Eastern Origin of the Tamils", Journal of Tamil Studies, no. 27, pp. 65-92.

_____. (1986). The Migration Routes of the Proto-Mande. The Mankind Quarterly, 7 (1), 77-96.

_____. (1986b). Dravidian Settlements in Ancient Polynesia. India Past and Present, (2), 225-241.

_____. (1988). "Common African and Dravidian Place Name Elements". South Asian Anthropologist, 9(1): 33-36.

_____. (1989a). "Tamil, Sumerian, Manding and the Genetic Model". International Journal of Dravidian Linguistics, 18 (1): 98-127.

_____. (1989b). "Review of Dr. Asko Parpola's 'The Coming of the Aryans'", International Journal of Dravidian Linguistics. 18(2): 98-127.

_____. (1990). "The Dravido-Harappan Colonization of Central Asia". Central Asiatic Journal, 34(1/2): 120-144.

_____. (1991). The Proto-Sahara". The Dravidian Encyclopedia. (Trivandrum: International School of Dravidian Linguistics) pp. 553-556. Volume 1.

_____. (1994). Afrocentricity: A valid frame of reference, Journal of Black Studies, ~5 (2) 170-190.

_____. (1994b). The Dravidian and African languages, International Journal of Dravidian Linguistics, 2~ (1), 34-52.

Yurco, F. (1989, September/October). "Were the Ancient Egyptians Black?" Biblical Archaeological Review. 15(5): 24-29.

Yurco, F. (1994). "How to teach ancient history: A multicultural model...And how not to." American Educator, (1), 34-38.

Thales of Miletus and Egypt
Theophile Obenga
San Francisco State University

Introduction

The general tradition of Western philosophy locates Thales as the first Greek philosopher and scientist. This supposition precludes an inquiry as to the source of his intellectual perspectives. According to ancient historical testimonia, Thales received his education from priests in the Nile Valley. These testimonia come from writers such as Diogenes Laertius, Plato, Aetius, Proclus, Iamblichus and Plutarch, among others. This essay, based on a very close scrutiny and exegesis of Greek texts, completely renews our understanding of Thales's association with Kemet.

Thales (The First Greek Philosopher and Scientist)

It is generally taught that Thales of Miletus (624-547 B.C.) was the first Greek philosopher and the founder of the Presocratic Ionian school in Asia Minor (Wheelwright, 1988, p. 40). It follows that Greek attempts to explain the world in truly rational terms began with the efforts of Thales and the other Milesian philosophers, Anaximander and Anaximenes. Accordingly, Western traditions of philosophy and science originate from them. Philip Wheelwright notes, "one of the great significant steps in the development of human thought took place at the Ionian city of Miletus in the sixth century B.C." (Wheelwright, 1988, p. 40). The advent of the Presocratic philosophers marked the rise of a nonmythopoetic way of thinking in Greece which eclipsed earlier concepts such as the naive Greek explanation of nature (physis) embraced by writers such as Homer *(Iliad and Odyssey)* and Hesiod *(Theogony)*. The inquiry into the causes *(aitia,* "a cause") of things first appears in Western intellectual history with Thales of Miletus. As Simplicius reports in his work *Physics.* "Thales is

165

traditionally the first *(protos)* to have revealed the investigation of nature *(paradedotai ten peri physeos)* to the Greeks" (Simplicius, p. 23, 29).

Thales, the first (protos) Greek scholar, received his training from Egyptian priests in the Nile Valley. This is clearly recorded by the Greeks themselves. It is equally clear from the known historical traditions of Greece *(akoe historein)* that Thales had no association whatsoever with Babylonia in Mesopotamia. The following excerpts comprise the corpus of ancient Greek testimonia with regard to the fruitful instruction received by Thales in Egypt.

Diogenes Laertius (Historian, third century A.D.)

"Thales, one of the so-called "Seven Sages," had no regular teacher in his life save for the priests of Egypt, under whom he studied (Diogenes, I, 27)":

Ïÿäåßò äÝ áýôï¼ êáèçôÞóáôï, ðëÞí äð åßò Á?õðôîï Ýëèùí ôïßò °åñåýóé óõíäéáôñéøáí

Clearly, then, Diogenes records that Thales of Miletus had never been taught by a master in Greece. Thales's pursuit of instruction saw him go by sea (pleo, "to sail") to Egypt, where he spent time with *(sun-diatribo)* the Egyptian priests *(tois hiereusi, dative case)*. This sentence is very limpid as well as actual in construction. We can then assume that Thales had traveled to Egypt for his education. Any speculation that this fact is doubtable belies the consideration that the Greeks were not inhibited about telling the truth as they observed it.

Plato (Philosopher, 428-347 B.C.)

Plato records that Thales was "educated in Egypt under the priests (Plato, X, 600)":

¸ðßßäåýèç Ýã ÁßåÝ ôôõ ýðü ôùí ßåñÝõþí

 166

The verb *paideuo* exactly means, "to bring up a child" (pais = "child"), "to train," "teach," or "educate." Here, the verb is used in the passive voice and the tense is <u>aorist</u> (as expressing past time). From this it is clear that when Thales went to Egypt, he had been as a child, lacking in knowledge, which placed him in the position to be taught, or " brought up as a child" by the Egyptian priests, who he came to revere. Cementing this proposition is the observation of the preposition h u p o, used with the genitive case, which means "under someone's power."

The Greek text does not present any type of ambiguity on the matter of Thales's status. There is no way to competently mistranslate it. Thales was well and truly indebted to Egypt for his education. According to Aetius, Thales studied philosophy in Egypt for a long enough period to be considered "an elder" when he returned (Aetius, I, 3, 1).

ÖéëïóïöÞóáò Ýí ÁßãýðÔòç Þëëáí åßò ÌßëçÔïí ðñåóñýóáññï The preposition *eis,* used with an accusative *only (eis Mileton)* creates the following basic sense: *into,* and then *to.* It is used here with the verb *erchomai (elthen),* which implies motion or direction. This verb, which means literally "to come" or "to go back, return," provides the meaning "then." That is, Thales then returned to Miletus, having studied philosophy in Egypt. The Greek text is very clear: Thales had been in Egypt, and then went back home. Moreover, the substantive *presbys* means "an old man" (Latin = *senex*). Here, the comparative *presbyteros* is formed from the substantive *presbys* (Smyth, 1920, 1984, p. 30).

G.S. Kirk and J.E. Raven did not translate Aetius's text with accuracy in their useful book *The Presocratic Philosophers.* Unfortunately, Kirk and Raven (1980, p. 76) write "Thales-having practiced philosophy in Egypt, came to Miletus when he was older.'" Upon close scrutiny, however, the sentence "when he was older" is not an accurate translation. For example: from a substantive (such as *basileus,* "king"), the Greek language can

167

form a comparative *(basileuteros,* "more kingly"). This is the grammatical case at present. Thales was not "older" in comparison to another person ("older than whom?" one might ask), but "more old," that is to say an elder when he went back to Miletus after having spent several years in Egypt for his education.

Thales had indeed become an elder--an old man with wisdom--under the direction of the Egyptian priests. To give further illustration, as we know, in the New Testament, *presbyteros* is used to refer to an elder of the Church *(presbyter)*. Armed with this experience, Thales naturally became founder of the first Greek school of philosophy and science. The verb *philosopheo* means literally in Greek, "to study" a thing, or "to philosophise." The verb is used above as an adjective-verbal noun (or a participle) in the aorist tense of the active voice *(philosophesas),* then, meaning "having studied philosophy steadily." This confirms what could be surmised from his eventual accomplishments: Thales was not a sluggish student. On the contrary, he took an active part in the study of philosophy under the authority of his Egyptian priest teachers.

The concept of philosophy embraces the pursuit of knowledge and wisdom as well as the acts of speculation, study and the investigation of truth and nature. Upon receiving instruction on the method of studying the nature of things and of truth in Egypt, Thales went back to his native city of Miletus as an elder, with knowledge and wisdom.

Proclus (Neoplatonist, 420-485 A.D.)

The science of geometry was invented in Egypt. This fact is recorded in Eudemus's *History of Geometry and Mathematics.* Having first (proton, "for the first time") been a student of Egyptian knowledge Thales transferred the speculative science of geometry to Greece (Proclus, 65, 3).

There were no methods of intellectual inquiry such as geometry in Greece before Thales's departure for Egypt. Upon his return, however, Thales introduced *(metegagen)* geometry in Greece. He had been taught this specific science in Egypt. We can observe the language used above: we have *ago,* which means literally "to carry, convey, or bring" and *meta* which means "back" or "after," as a preposition of sequence or succession This creates *metago,* which means "to convey from one place to another, to transfer, or introduce into."

The word *theoria,* strictly interpreted, means "that which a *theoros* does." A *theoros is* literally a "spectator," *so theoria* describes "the act of viewing" (Bill, 1901, pp. 196-204). As a question of science and intellectual activity, then, the noun *theoria* describes "speculation" or, more broadly, the conceptualization of a rational vision in the mind: intellectual sight and scientific knowledge. It is clear, then, that geometry was a matter of intellectual speculation in Egypt and, once again, the Greeks were honest in their appreciation.

The origins of geometry stretch far into classical Africa. Indeed, more than 1,000 years before Thales's birth, Egyptians had correctly calculated the areas of rectangles, triangles and isosceles trapeziums. The area of a circle had also been obtained accurately. Egyptians knew the rule for calculating the volume of a truncated pyramid. They also found the correct formula for the surface of a hemisphere.

Egyptian mathematical records, concentrated largely in primary documents such as the Rhind and Moscow Mathematical Papyri, also contain elements of trigonometry as well as a theory of similar triangles. In fact, Dr. George Abram Miller (1853-1951), who was a professor of Mathematics at the University of Illinois, devoted careful attention to the theoretical aspects of Egyptian mathematics in an article entitled "A Few Theorems Relating to the Rhind Mathematical Papyrus" (Miller, 1931, pp. 194-197). More recently, Hermann Engels of the Technical University of Aachen in Germany has demonstrated that the mathematicians of *ancient Egypt* approximated the area of a circle by a square with astonishing accuracy (Engels, 1977).

 169

The unduly unfavorable and derogatory assessment of ancient Egyptian mathematics must now be thrown away with all other similarly cultural prejudices. It has been shown that Thales studied rigorous geometry in ancient Egypt. It is a pity that some modern historiographers have continued to attempt to get rid of this historical fact, which was never questioned in antiquity.

In search of the ancient documentary support for this historical truth, we discover that there is a link between the fact that Thales was the first *(proton)* Greek student in Egypt and the fact that this same Thales first *(proton)* introduced philosophy and science in Greece (eis *ten* Hellada), having first come to Egypt to learn it (proton eis *Aigypton elthon)*.

Diogenes Laertius (Historian, third century A.D.) Thales, having studied geometry with the Egyptians, discovered for himself how to inscribe a right-angled triangle in a circle. Elated at this indication of his progress and mindful of tradition, he sacrificed an ox in thanksgiving.

Diogenes Laertius claims, citing Pamphile (Diogenes, I, 24), that Thales learned (manthano, "to learn by inquiry," "to learn how to do") from (para) Egyptians (Aigyption) how to practice geometry *(geometrein)*. The root of *manthano is math:* hence, *mathematics,* that is, all that is science, can only be learned from a teacher. Rhetoric and poetry are normally excluded from this Greek prerequisite of a teacher/pupil relationship. Having first studied geometry under the tutelage of the Egyptians, Thales was then able to profess geometry by himself, causing him to show his joy in a very expressive manner. Greek intellectual life really started with Thales, the Egyptian student. The Greeks never hid or minimized the historical truth, constantly pointing out the connection between the Egyptians, Thales and the Milesian school that he founded in the wake of his African educational experience.

Iamblicus (Neoplatonist philosopher, about 250-330 A.D.)

Pythagoras was born on the Ionian island of Samos around 572 B.C. He, like Thales, established a school of his own, choosing the city of Croton in southern Italy as the site of his institution. Also like Thales, Pythagoras traveled to Egypt to receive his basic education. Dr. Wheelwright observes that, "like many another ancient philosophers he [Pythagoras] journeyed in his youth to Egypt, where, for an indefinite number of years, he pursued studies in astronomy, geometry and theology under the tutelage of Egyptian priests" (Wheelwright, 1988, p. 200).

Why did Pythagoras go to Egypt? Thales strongly recommended that Pythagoras travel to Egypt and converse as often as possible with the priests of Memphis and Thebes (called Diospolis by the Greeks). Thales's counsel and advice carried great weight with Pythagoras; his experience with the Egyptian priests had elevated his reputation in Greece to that of a wise man and a scholar. Iamblicus reports that Thales urged Pythagoras to converse with the priests of Egypt (Iamblicus, 12). In fact, he used very emphatic Greek in saying this.

The adverb *malista* is the superlative of mala (very much). *Malista* therefore translates to "most of all," "above all," "for the most part," or "mostly." Thales advised Pythagoras to converse "most of all" (malista) with the Egyptian priests. Why? Reflecting on his experience of receiving instruction in the Nile Valley, Thales was counseling Pythagoras to seek out the wisest people he knew: the priests of Memphis and Thebes.

Generally, the verb *sum-ballo*, in the infinitive as *sum-balein*, means "to join or unite." The intransitive meaning of *sum-ballo* is "to come together or meet." Thales had recommended that above all, Pythagoras should meet the clergy of Memphis and Thebes in order to gain a higher level of knowledge. This is why, in pursuit of this higher education, Pythagoras spent over 22 years in Egypt among the priests.

The verb *dia-pleo* means "to sail across." Pythagoras, too, made his voyage to Egypt by sea. The Greek seashore station of Naucratis in the Nile Delta served as the primary contact point with Egypt, which was the fountainhead of Greek science. Thales himself (heauton), had received absolutely the same ("tauta", neuter plural), namely, education, knowledge and wisdom, from the Egyptian priests. Thales's advice to Pythagoras is not given in a passive or timid sense. The text uses the verb *pro-trepo*, "to urge on, impel or persuade" (one to do a thing), which is employed in the middle voice *(pro-etrepsato)*. In Greek, the middle voice usually denotes that the subject acts on himself or for himself. The aorist tense (here, *pro-etrepsato*) expresses, of course, the past tense. Thus, the sentence, translated precisely, means that Thales persuaded himself Pythagoras to sail across to Egypt (*dia-pleusai*, or "to have to go", an infinitive aorist, in the active voice).

It is quite clear, then, from the Greek text itself, that Thales acted on himself in persuading Pythagoras that he had to go to Egypt. Thales was intimately convinced (and therefore self-persuaded) that the Egyptian priests of Memphis and Thebes were excellent teachers. He was so convinced, in fact, that his conviction served as the persuading factor in Pythagoras's understanding of the beneficial education to be found in the Nile Valley.

Plutarch (Historian and Moralist, about 45-125 A.D.)

Thales's cosmology is known from his consideration of the proposition that the earth floats or rests on water (Aristotle, A3, 983b6). Thales held water *(to hudor)* to be the *arche,* or the first-principle and basic element *(stoicheion)* of all things. Diogenes Laertius writes "Thales laid it down that the first principle of all things is water" (Diogenes, I, 27). Consistent with their recognition of the source of most of their scientific knowledge, however, the Greeks explained that Thales (like Homer before him) made water the first-principle and the birth of all things as a result of being taught this by the Egyptians (Plutarch, 34).

Simplicius, the commentator on Aristotle, argues that Thales derived his ideas from views current in Egypt (Simplicius, 522, 14). The verb *oiomai* (participle form *oionta,* the accusative case) expresses a positive certainty when answering a question: "I believe," "of course," or "no doubt." The verb means "to think positively" or "to believe." The usage of this word indicates the fact that the Greeks held as a certainty the fact that Thales had traveled to Egypt for his instruction. Thales "made for himself" the (theory of) water as the principle of all things, although he had learned the doctrinal construct of the concept from the Egyptians.

Of course, in Egyptian cosmology, water (*mw* in Pharaonic language) played an essential part as the primeval slime *(nun)* out of which the world emerged. The Egyptian *nun* is both the first principle and the genesis of all things. According to the Egyptians, there existed in the beginning the *nun,* a primordial liquid mass in whose depths lay still the germs of all things. The spirit, or divine intelligence itself, emerges from the *nun* for the development of the universe.

To elevate an ordinary substance such as water to the status of the fundamental principle of all things is an example of philosophy at work, because it is an answer dealing with the world around us. More precisely, the utilization of water is a question of natural philosophy, or the attempt to place a single conception in a central position and to include in it all of the manifestations of nature. Max Planck writes that "it was in this way that Thales of Miletus[...]placed water[...]in the central position of the physical universe in which all physical facts are related and find an explanation" (Planck, 1925).

In the utilization of natural philosophy evident in the Egyptian concept of *nun,* physical and spiritual facts are tightly related; in other words, matter and spirit are not separated in a radical opposition. Being a fundamental principle of all things, nu*n* is also the ultimate explanation of the unity of the universe.

Diogenes Laertius (Historian, third century A.D.)

According to Hieronymus of Rhodes, who is quoted by Diogenes Laertius, Thales actually measured the pyramids by their shadow, having observed the time when a human being's shadow is equal to his height. Diogenes Laertius records the way this measurement was done, emphasizing that it was Thales himself who did it (Diogenes, I, 27). The middle voice aorist active infinitive *ekmetresai* means, "to measure for oneself." In this manner, Thales measured the pyramids for himself, by himself (autos, meaning "alone," "himself," "by himself"), by their shadow (ek *tens* skias). That these pyramids were in Egypt and not Greece should be beyond question: there are no pyramids in Greece. Plutarch and Pliny give the same basic account of Thales's pyramid measurements, carried out for himself and by himself. According to these writers, Thales obviously learned this technique from the Egyptians.

Aetius (Doxographer, about 100 A.D.)

Thales appears in Aetius Vetusta Placita or "Opinions") as the holder of a theory about the flooding of the Nile. According to Aetius, Thales speculates that the Etesian winds, blowing straight into the Nile Valley, cause the mass of the Nile's water to rise by cutting off its flow into the ocean, which has been swollen against its mouth (Aetius, IV, I, I).

Thales thinks (*oietai:*) without doubt, that the Etesian winds (*tous etesiasias a n e m o u s)* are the cause of the Nile flooding by preventing the river from running out into the sea. Herodotus had previously recorded a similar theory about the cause of the flooding of the Nile (Herodotus, II, 20). Thales could not make the computation of the height of pyramids from information received from Milesian traders who had visited the Nile Valley. Rather, Thales had seen the Nile himself, allowing him to advance his theory that the Etesian winds blow into Egypt as well and are the cause of the annual flooding of the Nile.

At no time, over the full length of their recorded history were the following facts ever debated by the Greek scholars themselves with regard to Thales:

1. Thales studied and practiced philosophy in Egypt *(philosophesas en Aigypto);*

2. Thales transferred Egyptian speculative geometry to Greece. *(metegagen ten theorian tauten eis ten Hellada).* This is not a question of the mere measurement of land mass; rather, it is the transmission of theoretical knowledge *(fheoria);*

3. Thales made water the first principle and birth of all things, having learned this natural philosophy from the Egyptians *(mathonta par' Aigyption). His* statements obviously mirror the role of *nun* in Egyptian cosmological theory.

4. Thales himself measured the pyramids by the height of his shadow *(ekmetresai auton tas pyramidas ek tens skias).* The fact that he personally made the trip to Egypt and took the measurements is reinforced by the fact that there are no pyramids in Greece.

5. Thales urged Pythagoras to sail across the sea to Egypt *(proetrepsato ton Pythagoran cis Aigypton diapleusai)* in order to get more knowledge from the Egyptian priests at Memphis and Thebes (Diospolis) than could be attained anywhere else. Memphis, or town of Ptah, sheltered a famous school of philosophy and science; likewise, Thebes, the city of Amun-Ra in Upper Egypt, was the site of an impressive academy of higher education.

6. Thales advanced a theory that the Etesian winds blow in Egypt as well as other places, and that they are the cause of the annual flooding of the Nile. (Thales *tous etesias anemous oietai...*) Thales (about 624-547 B.C.) was the founder of the Milesian school and intellectual and scientific life in Greece. Anaximander of Miletus (about 611-546 B.C.) was Thales's pupil and companion. Anaximenes (585-528 B.C.) was a disciple of Anaximander and a native of Miletus as well. Heraditus (born about 544 B.C.), was a native of Ephesus. The city of Ephesus lay about thirty miles north of Miletus. Anaxagoras (born about 500 B.C.) was a native of Clazomenae, not far from Heraclitus's native city of Ephesus. Pythagoras (born about 572 B.C.) was a native of Samos. He went to Egypt, upon the urging of Thales, and took with him three silver bowls as gifts for the priests. There, he learned the Egyptian language, so Antiphon tells us in his book *On Men of Outstanding Merit*.

The aforementioned cities, including Miletus, Ephesus, Clazonenae, Samos, Colophon, Cnidus, Cos (island), Chios (island), are Ionian cities in Asia Minor. Higher education in Greece, it can be safely surmised, started in Asia Minor, not at all in Europe with Athens or Sparta. In Ionia and, first of all in Miletus, Thales's native city, the wisdom of Egypt gave birth to Greek philosophy and science.

References

Aetius, I, 3, 1.

Aristotle, *Metaphysic*. A3, 983b6

Bill, Clarence P., "Notes on the Greek Èº?ðü¾ and Èº?ð³à," in *Transactions and Proceedings of the American Philological Association, Vol. IQCJGI (1901)*.

Diogenes Laertius, I. 27.

Engels, Heznsann, "Quadrature of the Circle in Ancient Egypt;' in Historia *Mathematica Vol.. 4 (May,* 1977).

Herodotus, II, 20

Iamblicus, *Vita Pytharorae, 12.*

Miller, G.A.. "A Few Theorems Relating to the Rhind Mathematical Papyrus," in *The American Mathematical Monthly, Vol. XGCVM, No. 4 (1931).*

Planck, Max. *A Survey of Physical Theory*. New York: Dover Publications (1993), p. 1 (First published, London, 1925).

Plato, *Republic*, X, 600A.

Plutarch, *Isis and Osiris*, 34.

Proclus, *On Euclid*. 65. 3.

Simplicius, *Physics*

Smyth, Herbert Weir, *Greek Grammar*. Cambridge, MA: Harvard University Press (1920, 1984).

Wheelwright. Philip. *The Presocratics*. New York: MacMillan Publishing Co (1988).

In the Final Analysis: Defending the Paradigm
Ama Mazama and Molefi Kete Asante

Clearly what the authors in this volume have suggested in one way or the other is that those who attack Afrocentric research and thinking often do not understand the basic paradigm. As has been discussed elsewhere, the idea of paradigm is central to an appreciation of the Afrocentric philosophy. (Mazama, 2001, p. 390) Inasmuch as the term paradigm has been applied to Afrocentricity by a number of our writers it is good to point out that the term remains ambiguous, yet it has some clear boundaries for the Afrocentrist. Kuhn (1962) borrowed the term from linguistics in order to demonstrate how a mode of scientific thought and practice could become institutionalized as an acceptable way of looking at the world.

What has been shown in this work, *Egypt vs. Greece and the American Academy*, is that there is a resistance in the academy to any realization of an African paradigm, that is, an African way of viewing reality or expressing cultural identity. American scholars like Mary Lefkowitz have sought to establish a White origin of civilization as well as to prevent the acceptance of an Afrocentric paradigm in cultural and historical studies. Equally, however, have been the Zuluean efforts of the Afrocentrists to establish the paradigm as a legitimate structure for understanding the history of Africa. We have begun to have a community of scholars who "practice the cognitive dimension of the paradigm" (Mazama, 2001, p. 391).

What has been re-confirmed by the authors of this volume is that during Pharaonic Egypt the classical civilization of Africa had no rival. It was the seminal culture of the period and all other civilizations, at the time, saw Egypt as the pinnacle of human achievement. If there was something special about Egypt, it existed in the variety of ways the ancient Africans confronted

 179

reality. Whether in art, sculpture, literature, astronomy, geometry, mathematics, law, politics, medicine, or architecture, the ancient Egyptians led the world. No amount of gainsaying by European triumphalists could defy the truth of Egypt's primacy during the Pharaonic era.

The abundant information in the ancient texts about the philosophers of Egypt, the literature of the age, the emphasis on the culture, and the nature of human beings relationship to each other readily affirm the significance of Egypt. One cannot underestimate the work of George G.M. James, Cheikh Anta Diop, and Chancellor Williams in providing the sources and the evidences with which our own authors have worked. They were the foundation scholars who laid the groundbreaking work that has been the chief source of the Eurocentrist's discomfort. Our task in this volume was to show that James and Diop and other scholars have stood on solid ground in their presentation of the ancient civilization. Although Egypt, Kemet, as we say, was not the only civilization of African antiquity, it was a society that brought many benefits to its people. Its policies, national and international, were designed to introduce the idea of communalism. No one could exist simply as an individual, all had to have community for national maturity. The fact that European scholars oppose this type of thinking suggests that they have not given up inserting Europe into our minds.

The fatal convulsion of the Eurocentrists means that the end is near for those who seek to uphold White racial domination. We know that it is necessary for the African community to start a national action committee devoted to the organizing principles of the Afrocentric movement. This is the only way that we will bring the total collapse of the Eurocentric assault on Afrocentricity. Vigilant scholars who will respond to the negative responses to our intellectual advances will be needed in the future. There is no end to the length and type of responses that the American academy's reactionaries will use to assault any position by an African scholar.

Our objective in this volume was to present an Africological discourse on the classical relationship between Egypt and Greece in a way that enlightened our readers. We have taken seriously the challenge from the Eurocentrists on the origin of civilization, the structure of knowledge in the American academy, and Egypt's influence on Greece. Molefi Kete Asante opens with an essay that discussed the issue of the Blackness of the ancient Egyptians. He argued that the question of the Blackness of the ancient Egyptians would never have been raised except for the persistent White racism in the academy. The issue did not appear before the 15th century and only became an issue with the vast discoveries in Egypt during the 19th century. Asante contends that racism was at the root of the color issue in regards to ancient Egyptians.

Concerned that the historiography of Africa was in the hands of Eurocentrists who were interested in promoting the idea that Africa had no history, Jacob Gordon argued that it was necessary to establish a new philosophy of writing African history. He stated that professional colonial historians believed firmly that African people had no history, or no history that they could study, or that was worth their studying.

Charles Finch tackled the thorny issue of historical evidences by critiquing the flaws in the work of Mary Lefkowitz. He interrogated the Greek sources and ancient historiography in order to understand why Lefkowitz misinterpreted or misunderstood the evidence of the ancients. He argued that Lefkowitz's assertion that we cannot rely on the evidence put forward by ancient writers means that we must jettison history itself. Finch appreciated the view that all historians of all times can be attacked and it can be said that no historian's evidence is credible because of some personal motivation. What Finch pointed out was that Lefkowitz

181

cross-examined her own witnesses and discredited them because she did not like their conclusions regarding ancient Egypt.

Asa Hilliard took Mary Lefkowitz to task for understating the arguments that opposed her position on the ancient Egyptian influence on Greece. He saw her work as incomplete, dishonest, and unscholarly. Hilliard demonstrated his contention by citing Lefkowitz's description of Cheikh Anta Diop as "Senegal's humanist and scientist." She failed to point out that Diop was immensely qualified to discuss the matters of history, which she challenged. Diop had formal training with the outstanding physicists and chemists of Europe. Furthermore, he was the director of the radio-carbon dating laboratory in Dakar, a fact that Lefkowitz did not mention in her book, *Not Out of Africa*.

In a determined bid to understand Mary Lefkowitz's distortion of the Afrocentric position on the history of ancient Africa, Charles Verharen sought to re-investigate the philosophical bases of Lefkowitz's book, *Not Out of Africa*. Verharen concluded that the consequences of Lefkowitz' position for African Americans was to dismiss the possibility of cultural or historical continuity in ways that do not occur when one speaks of the cultural continuity of Greek or Roman influences on contemporary Europe. Her work, according to Verharen, followed the same Eurocentric pattern of denying African contributions to world culture as other European scholars. Thus, the research philosophy articulated by Lefkowitz undermined the idea of African continuities as well as distorted the ancient picture of Nile Valley Civilization and its impact on Greece.

Don Luke spent considerable space detailing the relationship of ancient Africa to Scandinavia, pointing out with precision how Eurocentric writers, seeking to distance the influence of Africa on any part of Europe, constructed a twisted theory about the Black Scandinavians talked about in the Sagas. Luke wrote that it was predictable for Eurocentric scholars to try to gainsay the

182

evidence about Black Scandinavia because certain socio-cultural conclusions are prescribed. Europe must always appear superior and antecedent and Africa inferior and later. Luke called this the area where the theory takes precedence over the evidence.

Winters extended the arguments against the Eurocentric position by showing that Africans were not only the civilizers of Europe but that Africans were present in early Asia and may have been the progenitors of many Asian cultures. He argued that we must recognize African Egypt but also African Asia. Citing Cheikh Anta Diop, Winters established that Africans lived in West Asia in ancient times.

He outlined the rise of the Semitic race as a result of the mixing of Blacks in North Africa and West Asia with the Indo-European speaking Sea Peoples after 1300 B.C. He also pointed out that the archaeological evidence from Iraq and Iran suggested that the Elamites and Sumerians were Blacks.

In the final essay, Theophile Obenga located Thales of Miletus in the proper historical context in reference to the rise of philosophy. Although Thales is considered the father of Greek Philosophy and sometimes the father of philosophy, Obenga contended that it was impossible for Thales to have been the first philosopher since Thales was taught by African philosophers in Egypt. There was no way that the Greek student could have predated his African teachers. Positioning Thales as the "father of philosophy" as some European writers do is another way that history is turned on its head.

This volume has sought to bring this exceedingly competent group of scholars to the debate and discourse on the subject of Afrocentricity and the American Academy. We know that the issues of Egypt in Greece or Africans in Scandinavia or the origin of philosophy are central to the post-modern discourse on the nature of cultural reality. Our aim has been to set the record straight and at the same time to advance science.

183

Reference

Mazama, Ama (2001) "The Afrocentric Paradigm: Contours and Definitions," Journal of Black Studies, 31, 390-391.

ABOUT THE AUTHORS

Molefi Kete Asante is a Professor in the Department of African American Studies at Temple University and the creator of the first doctoral program in African American Studies. He received his doctorate from UCLA at the age of 26. Asante is the author of 51 books, including *The Egyptian Philosophers*, published by African American Images. Asante teaches ancient Egyptian language and culture at Temple University.

Ama Mazama is an Associate Professor in the Department of African American Studies at Temple University. She holds a Ph.D. in French from the Sorbonne where she graduated Magna Cum Laude. Dr. Mazama is the author of two books, more than two-dozen articles and reviews, and is considered one of the leading theorists of Afrocentricity. She has translated Afrocentricity into the French language. In addition, she has received two awards for outstanding scholarship and research from the Diop Conference Committee.

Charles Finch, MD, is Professor, School of Medicine at Morehouse University. The contributions of Charles Finch to the African origin of medicine are without peer. He is considered the most knowledgeable contemporary scholar dealing with the issues of African medicine in antiquity. His books on ancient Egypt are regularly consulted by other scholars because of their thoroughness.

Jacob Gordon is Professor of African Studies, University of Kansas in Lawrence, Kansas. Dr. Gordon has been a leading promoter of African Studies in the United States and Africa, having been one of the originators of the study of Africa at Kansas. He has written many articles and several books on the nature of African studies.

Asa Hilliard is the holder of the Distinguished Callaway Chair of Education at the Georgia State University in Atlanta. He was the Dean of Education at San Francisco State University prior to moving to Atlanta. Recognized as one of the foremost thinkers on African American pedagogy, Dr. Hilliard is an authority on ancient Egyptian history and culture and a long time student of the Egyptian language.

Don E. Luke teaches African American Studies at San Diego City College. He is one of the first people in the world to hold a doctorate in African American Studies, having received his Ph.D. at Temple University in 1991. Dr. Luke's work on the relationship of Africa to ancient Europe has produced numerous scholarly papers on the link between the ancient Africans and the Scandinavians. He is one of the few people in the world working on the transfer of ideas between Africa and Europe prior to the European Slave Trade.

Theophile Obenga is Professor and Chair, Department of Black Studies, San Francisco State University. He is the author of more than a dozen books on various scholarly topics related to African civilization. Trained in France and the United States, Dr. Obenga was a protégée of Cheikh Anta Diop and was lauded by his colleagues as the heir to Diop's mantle of scholarship.

Charles Verharen is Associate Professor, Department of Philosophy, Howard University. He has shown an interest in contemporary and classical African thought, from the emergence of Afrocentricity to the debate on the issues surrounding Diopian thought. Dr. Verharen is a frequent contributor to numerous journals, including the Journal of Black Studies.

Clyde Winters is the Director of the Uthman Dan Fodio Institute of Chicago and the author of scores of articles in international journals dealing with the African origin of civilization. Winters' work has been published in Asia, Europe, and the Americas. He has advanced the study of the cultural bases of knowledge in a series of powerful essays on the presence of Africans in India and other parts of Asia.